PENGUIN BOOKS

Biscuit & Slice

BIBLE

Biscuit & Slice

BIBLE

Introduction

Let's face it, everybody loves to indulge in a little tasty treat with their afternoon cup of tea or coffee, and nothing satisfies like a freshly baked biscuit or slice.

Home-baked biscuits and slices are quick to make, cheaper than their shop-bought cousins — and far tastier besides. Perfect for school lunchboxes, after-dinner treats, and any-time snacks, lovingly made fresh biscuits and slices also make a wonderful gift for friends and family.

All the recipes in this book are designed to be cooked in a standard home oven, with no need for fancy equipment or hard-to-find ingredients. The biscuits and slices range from old-fashioned family favourites to exotic offerings from abroad, plus some creative new suggestions that will get your taste buds tingling.

There's a mixture of sweet and savoury recipes, as well as no-bake and gluten-free options, so there's really something for everybody and every occasion.

Hints for baking biscuits and slices

CHOOSING A BAKING TIN

All the recipes included here give tin sizes where appropriate. Be aware that if using a larger tin than that specified, your slice will be thinner and take less time to cook. The opposite generally applies if using a smaller tin and you'll end up with a cakey result rather than a chewy one.

For uncooked slices, tin size generally doesn't matter and it is more a matter of personal preference.

GREASING TINS AND TRAYS

Clarified butter was traditionally used to grease trays, as it gives the best tasting results, but vegetable oil brushed (or sprayed) evenly will do almost as well and is easier for the busy home cook.

To use clarified butter, melt some butter slowly until it separates, then use a brush to spread the clear oil lightly over the tin or tray. Take care not to use the milky white solids, which can cause sticking (these should be discarded).

Whether using oil or clarified butter, it's important not to grease tins and trays too thickly, as this may actually cause the slice or biscuits to stick.

Lining tins and trays

If required to line a baking tin or tray, cut a strip of non-stick baking paper that covers the base and sides of the tin. Lightly grease the tin, place the paper inside, then brush or spray with oil, or brush with clarified butter. For slices, use a piece of baking paper that slightly overhangs the sides of the tin — this way you can grasp the baking paper to easily remove the slice after baking.

COOKING TIPS

- All cup and spoon measurements should be level, unless stated otherwise in the recipe.

- Always preheat the oven to the specified temperature before baking.

- Most biscuits work best if the dough is as soft as possible, so don't use too much flour on the board when rolling out. Or instead of using flour, roll dough between two sheets of baking paper or plastic wrap. Chill dough for at least 20 minutes before rolling out, to make it easier to handle.

- Place cut-out dough on chilled trays to prevent them spreading too much during cooking.

- Bright shiny trays cook more evenly than dark-coloured trays, which may cause biscuits to brown too quickly on the bottom. Line dark trays with heavy-duty foil to prevent this.

- Avoid using high-sided tins to cook biscuits as heat distribution is more uneven.

- Space trays of biscuits evenly throughout the oven, but be aware that most ovens cook unevenly to some degree. You may have to turn or swap the trays around during the cooking process so that all the biscuits are ready at the same time.

- Always cool biscuits on a wire rack after cooking, unless directed otherwise. Never overlap the biscuits when cooling, as they may end up misshapen.

- Butter is generally considered better for baking than margarine, but you can substitute one for the other if you wish.

- For better tasting biscuits and slices, use vanilla extract rather than its synthetic imitation, vanilla essence.

- Use butter, oil, margarine, milk and eggs at room temperature, unless otherwise specified.

- When oats are called for, make sure you use traditional rolled oats, not instant oats.

- When whisking egg whites into peaks, ensure that the bowl you are using is scrupulously clean and dry. When folding into a mixture, use a metal spoon.

STORAGE TIPS

- Always store biscuits and slices in an airtight container once cool.

- Store different types of biscuits in separate containers, so they keep their individual flavours.

- Biscuits that have softened can be crisped up by placing on an ungreased tray and heating in a moderate (180ºC) oven for several minutes.

- If you plan on serving a slice soon after baking, store it in the tin in which you baked it — covered in foil, after cooling and cutting.

Freezing tips

- Most biscuits and slices freeze well. Individual pieces of slice can be wrapped in plastic film and frozen ready for the lunchbox.

- Many biscuit doughs can also be successfully frozen and simply removed and cooked when required – perfect for unexpected visitors.

- Avoid icing slices and biscuits before freezing, as the icing may discolour or separate when defrosted. Instead, freeze un-iced and decorate once thawed.

Gluten-free flour

The gluten-free recipes included in this book require gluten-free flour. Gluten-free flour mixes are now available in many supermarkets, or from health food shops and specialist suppliers. However, you can also mix up your own – just make sure to store it in a sealed container in the freezer if only using occasionally.

The flours below are perfect for general baking of biscuits, slices and cakes.

General Purpose Gluten-free Flour Mix

175 g rice flour

100 g maize flour or dry polenta

175 g sorghum flour

Sweet Gluten-free Flour Mix 1

175 g rice flour

175 g cornflour

100 g fine potato flour

Sweet Gluten-free Flour Mix 2

250 g rice flour

250 g ground almonds

Abernethy biscuits

75 g cold butter, cut into small pieces

225 g plain flour

⅓ cup castor sugar

½ teaspoon baking powder

1 teaspoon caraway seeds

1 egg, beaten

1½ tablespoons milk

Preheat oven to 180°C. Lightly grease baking trays.

Combine butter and sifted flour in a food processor. Add sugar, baking powder and caraway seeds and blend. Mix the egg and milk together, then add them to the dry ingredients and process to combine.

Turn the dough onto a lightly floured surface. Roll it out thinly and cut into small rounds. Gather any leftover dough, roll out again and use to make more biscuits.

Transfer to prepared trays and bake for 10 minutes.

MAKES 40

Afghans

190 g softened butter

⅓ cup soft brown sugar

1¼ cups self-raising flour

2 tablespoons cocoa

1¾ cups Corn Flakes

chocolate glacé icing (page 241)

white chocolate buttons or walnut halves,
    for decorating (optional)

Preheat oven to 180°C. Lightly grease baking trays.

Cream butter and sugar, then add sifted flour and cocoa. Carefully stir
in the Corn Flakes a little at a time.

Drop spoonfuls of mixture onto the trays and bake for 12–15 minutes.

When completely cooled, ice with chocolate icing. Top each biscuit with
a white chocolate button or walnut half, if desired.

MAKES 24

Almond biscotti

2 cups plain flour

1½ teaspoons baking powder

½ teaspoon ground cinnamon

¾ cup white sugar

1½ cups whole raw almonds

3 eggs

2 teaspoons vanilla extract

Preheat oven to 180°C. Lightly grease baking trays.

In a large bowl, combine sifted flour, baking powder and cinnamon, and sugar. Add almonds and mix to combine.

In a small bowl, whisk together the eggs and vanilla. Fold egg mixture into flour mixture until a stiff dough forms.

Turn dough onto a lightly floured surface and divide into two pieces. Roll each piece into a log about the same length as your baking tray. Place the logs on the baking tray, leaving plenty of room between them, and flatten slightly. Bake for 25 minutes.

Remove from the oven (leave the oven on) and set aside until cool enough to handle. >

Using a serrated knife, slice each log diagonally into 1-cm thick slices.

Return biscuits to the tray and bake for a further 12–15 minutes, until crisp.

VARIATIONS
For anise biscotti, replace the vanilla extract with anise extract and omit the almonds. For chocolate almond biscotti, replace the vanilla extract with almond extract and add ¼ cup cocoa to the flour mix.

MAKES 40

Almond biscuits

100 g softened butter
⅓ cup white sugar
1 cup ground almonds
⅔ cup gluten-free flour mix (page xiii)
1 egg, separated
½ cup almonds, chopped

Preheat oven to 180°C.

Cream butter and sugar until light and fluffy. Add ground almonds and sifted flour and mix well.

Reserve a little of the egg white, then beat the rest of the egg and add to the mixture to form a firm dough.

Roll dough out to a thickness of 3 mm and cut into rounds or shapes using a biscuit cutter.

Brush biscuits with reserved egg white and sprinkle with chopped almonds.

Cook for 10–12 minutes or until golden.

MAKES 24 | GLUTEN FREE

Almond lace doilies

80 g butter, melted

½ cup finely ground almonds

3 tablespoons plain flour

½ cup white sugar

2 tablespoons sour cream

½ teaspoon vanilla extract

Preheat oven to 180°C. Lightly grease baking trays.

Grind the almonds in a food processor until finely ground (or chop very finely).

Place the melted butter in a large bowl and add the ground almonds, sifted flour, sugar, cream and vanilla. Mix well.

Drop teaspoonfuls of the mixture onto prepared trays and bake for 10 minutes, or until golden.

Cool on the trays for a few moments, then gently transfer to a wire rack to cool completely.

MAKES 16

Almond shortbread

300 g softened butter
½ cup castor sugar
1½ cups plain flour
1½ cups rice flour
½ cup ground almonds
a few drops almond essence
blanched almonds, for decorating

Cream butter and sugar until light and fluffy. Sift the flours together and gradually stir into butter mixture.

Add ground almonds and almond essence and mix until smooth.

Refrigerate dough for 30 minutes.

Preheat oven to 150°C. Lightly grease a baking tray.

Divide dough into 4 pieces and roll out on a lightly floured surface to make 4 rounds, each about 1.5 cm thick. Pinch edges and cut each round into 8 triangular pieces. Sprinkle with blanched almonds.

Bake for 20–30 minutes or until shortbread just begins to colour (be careful it doesn't burn). Let cool on the tray for 5 minutes before transferring to a wire rack.

MAKES 32

Amaretti

1 cup ground almonds

1 cup castor sugar

2 egg whites

½ teaspoon vanilla extract

a few drops almond essence

blanched almonds, split in half, for decorating

Preheat oven to 180°C. Lightly grease baking trays and dust with flour.

Combine ground almonds and sugar. Add egg whites, vanilla extract and almond essence. Beat with an electric mixer on medium speed for 3 minutes, until light and fluffy.

Spoon mixture into a piping bag fitted with a 1-cm round tip and pipe biscuits onto baking trays. Use a circular motion, starting from the centre, to make biscuits 4-cm in diameter.

Top each biscuit with half an almond, and bake for 12 minutes or until tops are lightly browned.

MAKES 20 | GLUTEN FREE

American tollhouse cookies

2¼ cups plain flour

1 teaspoon bicarbonate of soda

1 teaspoon salt

160 g softened butter

¾ cup white sugar

¾ cup soft brown sugar,
firmly packed

1 teaspoon vanilla extract

2 eggs

2 cups chocolate chips

1 cup chopped pecans or walnuts

Preheat oven to 180°C.

Sift together flour, bicarbonate of soda and salt.

In a separate bowl, cream butter, sugars and vanilla until light and creamy.
Beat in eggs.

Gradually add flour mixture to butter mixture, mixing until well combined.
Stir in chocolate chips and nuts.

Drop teaspoonfuls of dough onto ungreased baking trays, leaving plenty
of room for spreading. Bake for 8–10 minutes.

MAKES 60

Animal biscuits

½ cup wholemeal flour

1 cup plain flour

¼ teaspoon ground ginger

¼ teaspoon ground cinnamon

pinch of salt

⅔ cup semolina

75 g cold butter, cut into
small pieces

1 ripe banana

1½ tablespoons maple syrup

cream cheese or icing (pages
241–44), to frost

sultanas or chocolate chips,
for decorating

Preheat oven to 200°C. Lightly grease baking trays.

Sift together flours, spices and salt. Stir in semolina. Rub in butter with your fingertips until crumbly. Mash the banana with the maple syrup and stir into the flour mixture to make a smooth, pliable dough.

Roll out dough on a floured surface and cut into animal shapes with biscuit cutters. Gather any leftover dough, roll out again and use to make more biscuits. Bake for 20 minutes, or until golden and firm.

Cool on a wire rack. Frost with cream cheese that has been beaten with a little icing sugar, or top with coloured icing. Score the frosting with a fork to make it look like fur. Use sultanas or choc chips for eyes.

MAKES 15–20

Anzac biscuits

100 g butter, melted

2 tablespoons boiling water

1 teaspoon bicarbonate of soda

2 tablespoons golden syrup

1 cup plain flour

1 cup white sugar

2 cups rolled oats

¾ cup desiccated coconut

Preheat oven to 190°C. Lightly grease baking trays.

Mix together butter, boiling water, bicarbonate of soda and golden syrup.

In a separate bowl, mix the sifted flour, sugar, oats and coconut. Add the liquid and blend until well combined.

Drop spoonfuls of mixture onto trays and cook for 10–12 minutes, or until golden.

MAKES 30

Anzac slice

1 cup rolled oats

1½ cups plain flour

1 cup soft brown sugar, firmly
   packed

1 cup desiccated coconut

finely grated zest of 1 orange

125 g butter

2 tablespoons golden syrup

2 tablespoons orange juice

½ teaspoon bicarbonate of soda

½ cup marmalade

Preheat oven to 180°C. Grease and line a 19-cm × 29-cm slice tin.

Combine oats, sifted flour, sugar, coconut and orange zest in a large bowl.
Mix well.

Place butter, golden syrup and orange juice in a saucepan and stir over
low heat, without boiling, until the butter has melted. Bring to the boil,
then remove from heat and stir in the bicarbonate of soda.

Add liquid to dry ingredients and stir well to combine.

Press two-thirds of the mixture into the tin, then spread evenly with
marmalade. Crumble remaining mixture over the top.

Cook for about 35 minutes, or until golden brown. Cool for 5 minutes
in the tin, then transfer to a wire rack to cool. Cut into squares.

MAKES 36

Apple and date chews

450 g apples, peeled and chopped

75 g mixed nuts, chopped

1 cup dates, chopped

1 cup gram flour (besan)

½ cup castor sugar

2 tablespoons butter, melted

1 tablespoon honey

1 egg, beaten

pinch of salt

Preheat oven to 180°C. Grease and line a 19-cm × 29-cm slice tin.

Mix all the ingredients together until well combined. Spread into the tin.

Bake for 20–30 minutes until golden brown. Cool in the tin, then cut into fingers before turning out.

MAKES 30 | GLUTEN FREE

Apricot almond slice

1 cup self-raising flour

125 g cold butter, cut into small pieces

½ cup white sugar

1 egg, beaten

apricot jam, for spreading

milk, to brush

½ cup chopped almonds

Preheat oven to 180°C. Lightly grease a 19-cm square cake tin.

Rub butter into sifted flour until crumbly, then add sugar. Add egg and mix to form a stiff dough.

Turn onto a lightly floured surface and knead gently. Divide dough into two pieces. Roll out one piece to just fit cake tin, and press into tin. Spread with apricot jam.

Roll out remaining dough and place on top. Brush with milk and sprinkle with chopped almonds.

Bake for 20–30 minutes. Cover with foil if the almonds start to burn.

MAKES 16

Apricot and sesame slice

2 tablespoons butter

2 tablespoons golden syrup

2 tablespoons soft brown sugar

⅓ cup desiccated coconut

100 g rice flakes (precooked
variety)

⅓ cup chopped dried apricots

2 tablespoons sesame seeds

½ teaspoon ground cinnamon

pinch of salt

¼ cup milk chocolate chips

Preheat oven to 150°C. Grease and line a 19-cm × 29-cm slice tin.

Melt the butter and golden syrup over a low heat. Mix all the other ingredients (except choc chips) together in a bowl, then stir in the melted butter and syrup. Mix in the chocolate chips.

Press mixture firmly into the tin. Bake for 30–35 minutes.

Cool in the tin before cutting into squares or fingers and turning out.

MAKES 24 | GLUTEN FREE

Apricot, ginger and lemon slice

¾ cup dried apricots

1½ cups self-raising flour

pinch of salt

½ teaspoon ground cinnamon

125 g cold butter, cut into small
    pieces

1½ cups white sugar

¼ cup preserved ginger,
    chopped

¼ cup walnuts, chopped

1 egg

½ cup milk

lemon glacé icing (page 241)

Soak apricots in warm water for 30 minutes, then drain and chop.

Preheat oven to 180°C. Lightly grease and line a 19-cm × 29-cm slice tin.

Sift together flour, salt and cinnamon. Rub in butter with your fingertips until crumbly. Add sugar, apricots, ginger and nuts and mix until combined.

Beat together egg and milk, then add to mixture and stir until well combined.

Spread mixture into tin and bake for 25–30 minutes.

When cool, top with lemon icing and once set, cut into fingers.

MAKES 36

Apricot hazelnut crunch

250 g white vegetable shortening, chopped

250 g dried apricots, finely chopped

125 g hazelnuts, finely chopped

3 cups Corn Flakes

1¼ cups desiccated coconut

¾ cup white sugar

¼ cup full-cream milk powder

Grease and line a 19-cm × 29-cm slice tin.

Heat shortening gently until just melted. Add to remaining ingredients and stir until well combined.

Press mixture into tin. Refrigerate for at least 2 hours, then cut into bars.

MAKES 24 | NO BAKE

Apricot lunchbox biscuits

1½ cups plain flour

1 teaspoon baking powder

1 teaspoon ground cinnamon

1 cup rolled oats

½ cup soft brown sugar

¾ cup dried apricots, chopped

1 tablespoon flaked almonds

⅔ cup natural yoghurt

3 tablespoons canola oil

soft brown sugar, for sprinkling

Preheat oven to 190°C. Lightly grease a baking tray.

Sift together the flour, baking powder and cinnamon. Stir in the other dry ingredients.

In a separate bowl, beat together the yoghurt and oil. Add to the dry ingredients and mix to make a firm dough.

Roll the mixture into about 16 balls, place on prepared baking tray and flatten slightly with a fork. Bake for 15–20 minutes, until golden brown and firm to the touch.

MAKES 16

Apricot meringue slice

175 g softened butter

½ cup white sugar

2 egg yolks

1 cup self-raising flour

1 cup plain flour

4 tablespoons milk

1 teaspoon of vanilla extract

apricot jam, for spreading

2 egg whites

1 cup castor sugar

1 cup desiccated coconut

Preheat oven to 180°C. Lightly grease a 23-cm square slab tin.

For the base, cream butter and sugar until light and fluffy, then beat in egg yolks. Add sifted flours, milk and vanilla and mix well.

Press into prepared tin and spread with jam.

For the topping, beat egg whites and sugar until stiff peaks form. Carefully fold in coconut. Spread over the base and bake for 30 minutes, making sure the meringue doesn't burn.

When cold, cut into squares.

MAKES 16

Apricot turnover biscuits

100 g softened unsalted butter

¾ cup castor sugar

2 eggs, lightly beaten

2⅔ cups self-raising flour

1 teaspoon ground cloves

1 × 400-g tin apricots (or peaches or pie apples)

1½ tablespoons soft brown sugar

2 tablespoons castor sugar mixed with 1 teaspoon ground cinnamon, for sprinkling

ICING

3 cups icing sugar

⅓ cup boiling water

Cream butter and sugar until light and fluffy. Add eggs one at a time, beating well after each addition.

Add sifted flour and cloves and mix to form a soft dough. Turn onto a floured surface and knead gently. Cover with plastic film and chill for at least 20 minutes.

Preheat oven to 180°C. Line baking trays with baking paper.

Divide dough into 2 pieces. Roll out each piece to about 5 mm thick. Using a 9-cm biscuit cutter, cut 11 rounds from the first piece of dough. Using an 8-cm biscuit cutter, cut another 11 rounds from the second piece of dough.

Drain and purée the tinned apricots, then place a tablespoon of the purée on each of the smaller rounds, leaving a border around the edge. Sprinkle over some of the brown sugar. Top with the larger rounds, pressing edges together to seal.

Bake for 15 minutes, or until lightly browned. Let biscuits cool on trays for 5 minutes before transferring to a wire rack.

For the icing, sift icing sugar into a bowl. Stir in boiling water until smooth. Spoon icing over biscuit tops and sprinkle with cinnamon sugar.

MAKES 10

Auntie Ruth's lemon slice

BASE

1½ cups Corn Flakes, crushed

120 g butter, melted

¼ cup white sugar

TOPPING

1 × 395-g tin condensed milk

½ cup lemon juice

finely grated zest of 1 lemon

1 egg yolk

Lightly grease a 23-cm square slice tin.

For the base, mix all ingredients together. Press into the tin. Refrigerate for about 10 minutes.

For the topping, beat ingredients together until thick and fluffy. Pour evenly over base. Return to refrigerator until set, then cut into slices.

MAKES 36 | NO BAKE

Bagel biscuits

1 × 25-g sachet dried yeast

½ teaspoon sugar

1 cup lukewarm water

3 cups plain flour

180 g cold butter, cut into
small pieces

1 teaspoon salt

1 tablespoon olive or vegetable oil

½ teaspoon ground cumin or
coriander (optional)

sesame seeds, for coating

In a small bowl, dissolve the yeast and sugar in some of the lukewarm water and set aside for 10 minutes.

Sift flour into a bowl and make a well in the middle. Add butter, salt, oil, yeast mixture, remaining water and spice (if using).

Knead to a soft, smooth dough and leave in a warm place to rise for 1 hour.

Preheat oven to 190°C. Lightly grease baking trays.

Divide the dough into about 30 pieces, and shape each into a thin log about 10 cm long. Roll each log in sesame seeds to coat. Pinch the ends of each log together to form a ring.

Place 'bagels' on baking trays and bake for 45 minutes, or until brown.

MAKES 30

Banana nut biscuits

125 g softened butter
½ cup soft brown sugar
½ cup peanut butter
½ cup mashed banana
1 cup self-raising flour
pinch of salt

Cream butter and sugar until light and fluffy. Add peanut butter and banana and mix well.

In a separate bowl, sift together dry ingredients. Add to banana mixture, and stir well to combine.

With floured hands, roll mixture into long logs, about 3-cm in diameter. Wrap in foil and chill until cold. (Alternatively, drop dessertspoonfuls of mixture onto greased baking trays.)

Preheat oven to 180°C. Lightly grease baking trays.

Cut the logs into 8-mm slices, then transfer to baking trays and bake for 12–15 minutes.

MAKES 40

Billionaire shortbread bars

100 g softened butter

¼ cup castor sugar

1½ cups self-raising flour

75 g white cooking chocolate

75 g dark cooking chocolate

125 g butter

½ cup castor sugar

2 tablespoons golden syrup

1 × 395-g tin condensed milk

Preheat oven to 180°C. Grease and line a 19-cm × 29-cm slice tin.

For the base, cream butter and sugar until light and fluffy. Fold in sifted flour. Press mixture evenly into base of tin. Bake for 15 minutes or until golden. Set aside to cool.

For filling, combine butter, sugar, golden syrup and condensed milk in a saucepan. Stir over low heat until dissolved, then boil for several minutes, stirring vigorously, until caramel in colour. Spread over cooked base and leave to cool.

For the topping, melt white and dark chocolate separately, in a double boiler or on MEDIUM in the microwave. Pour over the slice one at a time, spreading evenly. Use a fork to create a swirly pattern through the chocolate.

MAKES 16

Blackberry lattice fingers

1½ cups plain flour

½ teaspoon baking powder

125 g cold butter, cut into small pieces

½ cup castor sugar

½ teaspoon vanilla extract

1 egg, beaten

¼ cup blackberry jam (or other fruit jam)

Preheat oven to 180°C. Lightly grease a 19-cm × 29-cm baking tray.

Sift together flour and baking powder. Add butter and rub in with your fingertips until crumbly. Stir in sugar and vanilla and add enough egg to work into a dough.

Knead dough lightly on a floured surface. Roll out two-thirds of the dough to make a rectangle about 18-cm × 28-cm in size. Place on the prepared tray and spread evenly with the jam.

Roll remaining dough into an 18-cm square. Cut into 1.5-cm strips with a sharp knife and place in a lattice pattern over the jam.

Bake for about 25 minutes or until golden brown. Cool and then cut into fingers.

MAKES 20

Bran biscuits

1 cup wholemeal flour

1 teaspoon baking powder

2 cups unprocessed (natural) bran

⅓ cup castor sugar

125 g cold butter, cut into small pieces

2 eggs, lightly beaten

Preheat oven to 180°C.

Sift together flour and baking powder. Mix in bran and sugar, then rub butter through dry ingredients with your finger tips. Add eggs and mix in thoroughly with a fork.

Turn mixture onto a lightly floured surface and knead gently into a smooth dough.

Roll dough out thinly and cut into strips or squares. Prick all over with a fork.

Bake for 10–15 minutes or until golden brown.

MAKES 36

Brandy snaps

1 cup plain flour

1 teaspoon ground ginger

½ teaspoon ground cinnamon

100 g butter

⅓ cup golden syrup

½ cup castor sugar

1 tablespoon brandy

Preheat oven to 160°C. Line baking trays with baking paper.

Sift together the flour, ginger and cinnamon.

Place the butter, golden syrup and sugar into a saucepan over medium heat and stir until the butter has melted. Simmer for 1 minute, then add to the dry ingredients. Stir well, then mix in the brandy.

Drop tablespoons of the mixture onto trays, leaving 4 cm between each to allow for spreading.

Bake for 15–18 minutes or until golden. Cool for 5 minutes on the trays before transferring to a wire rack.

Allow to cool flat, or, while still warm, roll around the handle of a large wooden spoon to form a tube. Remove from handle while still warm, then allow to cool. Fill tubes with sweetened whipped cream or your choice of filling.

MAKES 18

Butterscotch brownies

125 g soft brown sugar

125 g softened butter

2 eggs, beaten

1 teaspoon vanilla extract

¾ cup self-raising flour

50 g walnuts, chopped

Preheat oven to 170°C. Lightly grease an18-cm square baking tin.

Cream butter and sugar until light and fluffy. Beat in eggs and vanilla, then gently fold in sifted flour. Add the walnuts and mix well.

Pour mixture into tin and bake for 35–40 minutes. Cut into squares when cool.

MAKES 16

Butterscotch date biscuits

125 g softened butter

2 cups soft brown sugar, firmly packed

2 eggs, beaten

1 teaspoon vanilla extract

3½ cups plain flour

½ teaspoon salt

1 teaspoon bicarbonate of soda

1 teaspoon baking powder

FILLING

500 g dates, chopped

½ cup soft brown sugar

½ cup water

½ cup blanched almonds, chopped

Cream butter and sugar until light and fluffy. Add eggs and vanilla and beat well. Sift together all dry ingredients, then add to creamed mixture and stir until thoroughly combined. Roll the dough into a log about 4 cm in diameter, wrap in foil and refrigerate for several hours, until cold. Preheat oven to 180°C. Lightly grease baking trays.

For the filling, heat dates, sugar and water in a saucepan until thickened. Stir in nuts.

Cut the log into slices. Place half the slices on greased baking trays. Top each with a dollop of the date filling and place a second slice of dough on top. Press edges together with a fork to seal.

Bake for about 10 minutes, or until lightly browned.

MAKES 60

Caramel crackle squares

250 g jersey caramels, chopped

1 tablespoon golden syrup

60 g butter

250 g dark cooking chocolate, chopped

3 cups Rice Bubbles

100 g white marshmallows, chopped

Grease and line a 23-cm square slab tin.

Put caramels, golden syrup, butter and half the chocolate in a bowl. Microwave on MEDIUM for 2 minutes, then stir until smooth. Mix in Rice Bubbles.

Press into prepared dish.

Put remaining chocolate and marshmallows in a bowl. Microwave on MEDIUM for 45 seconds, then stir until smooth. Spread over the caramel mixture. Leave to set then cut into small squares.

MAKES 36

Caramel-crusted fruit slice

125 g butter

1 cup soft brown sugar

1 egg, lightly beaten

225 g mixed dried fruit

150 g self-raising flour

Preheat oven to 180°C. Lightly grease a 19-cm × 29-cm slice tin.

Melt butter in a large saucepan. Add sugar, and stir over low heat until dissolved. Remove from heat and cool for a few minutes so egg doesn't scramble when added. Stir in egg, then add fruit and sifted flour. Mix well.

Press into baking tin and bake for 20 minutes, or until a crust has formed but the centre is still not completely set. Be careful not to overcook or the slice will be crisp and biscuit-like, rather than chewy.

Cool slightly and score 4 cm squares with a sharp knife. Allow to cool completely in the tray, then cut into squares.

MAKES 24

Caramel slice

1 cup self-raising flour

½ cup white sugar

½ cup desiccated coconut

½ cup Corn Flakes

125 g butter

1 × 395-g tin condensed milk

2 tablespoons golden syrup

2 tablespoons butter

1 tablespoon sugar

3 tablespoons white vegetable shortening

½ cup drinking chocolate powder

Preheat oven to 180°C. Lightly grease a 19-cm × 29-cm slice tin.

For the base, sift flour into a bowl, then mix in sugar, coconut and Corn Flakes. Melt butter, pour over dry ingredients and mix well.

Press into tin and bake for 10 minutes.

For the filling, put all ingredients in a saucepan and boil for 10 minutes, stirring constantly. Pour over the base.

For the topping, melt vegetable shortening and mix in sifted drinking chocolate. Pour over the caramel layer, and leave to set. Cut into squares or fingers when cold.

MAKES 36

Caraway crisps

½ cup softened butter

1 cup cream cheese

¼ cup white sugar

1 cup self-raising flour

¼ teaspoon salt

2 tablespoons caraway seeds

1 tablespoon sea salt

Cream butter and cream cheese until smooth, then add the sugar. Gradually stir in sifted flour and salt.

Roll dough into logs 5-cm in diameter, wrap in foil and chill for at least 30 minutes.

Preheat oven to 220°C. Lightly grease baking trays.

Cut logs into thin slices, place on baking trays and sprinkle with caraway seeds and sea salt.

Bake for about 6 minutes, or until golden and crisp.

MAKES 40

Cath's poppy seed slice

240 g butter

1 cup white sugar

2 eggs, beaten

6 heaped tablespoons poppy
seeds

juice and grated zest of 1 lemon

1 tablespoon wholemeal flour

$1\frac{1}{2}$ cups plain flour

1 tablespoon custard powder
or cornflour

1 teaspoon baking powder

$\frac{1}{2}$ cup chopped walnuts, toasted

$\frac{1}{2}$ cup sultanas

icing sugar, for dusting

Preheat oven to 180°C. Lightly grease a 19-cm × 29-cm slice tin or small roasting pan.

Melt butter in a large saucepan. Add sugar and dissolve over low heat. Remove from heat and cool for a few minutes so eggs don't scramble when added. Stir in eggs, then poppy seeds, lemon zest and juice. (For a lighter slice, grind the poppy seeds first.)

In a separate bowl sift together the flours, custard powder or cornflour and baking powder. Stir into the egg mixture, followed by the nuts and sultanas. Mix well.

Pour into the prepared tray. Bake for 45 minutes. Let cool a little, but cut into squares while still warm. When cold, dust with icing sugar.

MAKES 36

Cheese-cream sandwiches

1½ cups plain flour

½ teaspoon turmeric

2 teaspoons curry powder

¼ teaspoon freshly ground black
   pepper

¼ teaspoon salt

125 g cold butter, cut into small
   pieces

¼ cup finely grated cheddar
   cheese

1 egg yolk

3 teaspoons cold water

paprika, for sprinkling

FILLING

60 g cream cheese

¼ cup finely grated cheddar
   cheese

2 tablespoons finely grated
   parmesan cheese

freshly ground black pepper

Preheat oven to 180°C. Lightly grease baking trays.

Sift together flour, turmeric, curry powder, pepper and salt. Using your fingertips, rub in the butter until the mixture is crumbly. Add cheese and mix to just combine.

Add egg yolk and water and mix to a firm dough.

Turn out onto floured surface and knead lightly. Roll out dough to 3 mm in thickness. Cut into rounds with a 4-cm biscuit cutter.

Place rounds onto baking trays. Bake for 8–10 minutes or until light golden.

For the filling, beat cream cheese until soft and smooth. Add cheddar and parmesan and season to taste with pepper. Beat again until soft and spreadable.

When biscuits are cold, sandwich together with the cheese cream. Sprinkle tops with paprika.

MAKES 20

Cheese straws

⅓ cup plain flour
pinch of salt
pinch of cayenne pepper
60 g cold butter, cut into small pieces
½ cup grated tasty cheese
1 egg yolk
1 teaspoon lemon juice

Preheat oven to 180°C. Lightly grease baking trays.

Sift together flour, salt and cayenne pepper. Rub in the butter
with your fingertips until crumbly.

Add grated cheese, then mix in the egg yolk and lemon juice to form a
pliable dough.

Roll dough out thinly on a lightly floured surface and cut into thin strips.
(Use a fluted pastry cutter to create a ruffled edge.) Place on trays and
bake for 6 minutes, or until golden brown.

Serve cheese straws on their own, or with dip.

MAKES 24–36

Cherry coconut crisps

125 g softened butter

1½ tablespoons icing sugar

½ teaspoon vanilla extract

1 egg yolk

1 cup plain flour

pinch of salt

2 tablespoons desiccated coconut
(or use coconut flakes)

¼ cup glacé cherries, chopped

Cream the butter and icing sugar until light and fluffy. Add the vanilla and egg yolk and beat well.

Sift together the flour and salt and stir into the creamed mixture, followed by the coconut and cherries.

Roll mixture into a long log about 5 cm in diameter. Wrap tightly in foil and chill in the refrigerator until cold.

Preheat oven to 180°C. Lightly grease baking trays.

Cut refrigerated dough into thin slices, place on baking trays and bake for 12–15 minutes or until golden

(This biscuit dough can be stored in the refrigerator for up to 2 weeks, or frozen for 2 months.)

MAKES 36

Cherry macaroons

2 egg whites

100 g ground almonds

¾ cup castor sugar

2 tablespoons white sugar

glacé cherries, for decorating

Preheat oven to 180°C. Lightly grease baking trays.

Beat egg whites until thick. Gently fold in remaining ingredients (except cherries).

Pipe or spoon the mixture onto prepared trays, leaving plenty of space for spreading. Top each biscuit with a glacé cherry.

Bake for 10–15 minutes, until light brown – remove from the oven as soon as they start to change colour, as they burn easily.

MAKES 24 | GLUTEN FREE

Chocká cherry bars

BASE

1 cup icing sugar

2 tablespoons cocoa

2 cups Rice Bubbles

125 g butter, melted

TOPPING

2 cups desiccated coconut

½ cup icing sugar

125 g glacé cherries, chopped

2 egg whites

Grease and line a 19-cm × 29-cm slice tin.

For the base, sift together icing sugar and cocoa, then stir in Rice Bubbles. Add melted butter and mix until well combined.

Press mixture into the tin. Refrigerate until set.

For the topping, combine coconut, sifted icing sugar and cherries in a bowl. Add unbeaten egg whites and mix well.

Spread topping evenly over the base. Refrigerate several hours or overnight. Cut into bars to serve.

MAKES 24 | NO BAKE

Chocolate chip cookies

125 g softened butter

½ cup soft brown sugar

¼ cup white sugar

1 teaspoon vanilla extract

1 egg

1 cup plain flour

½ teaspoon bicarbonate of soda

pinch of salt

¾ cup chocolate chips

Cream butter and sugars until light and fluffy. Add vanilla and egg and beat until combined.

Sift together flour, bicarbonate of soda and salt and stir into creamed mixture. Add chocolate chips and mix well.

Roll mixture into a log about 5 cm in diameter, then wrap in plastic film and freeze for 1–2 hours.

Preheat oven to 190°C. Lightly grease baking trays.

Remove dough from freezer and thaw for 10 minutes before cutting into 1 cm slices. Place slices on baking trays and bake for 10–12 minutes, until golden brown.

MAKES 36

Chocolate diamonds

60 g dark cooking chocolate

120 g butter

1 cup castor sugar

2 eggs

1 teaspoon vanilla extract

½ cup plain flour

¾ cup chopped walnuts

Preheat oven to 200°C. Lightly grease a 25-cm × 30-cm Swiss roll tin and dust with flour.

Melt chocolate and butter together in a double boiler over simmering water, or on MEDIUM in the microwave. Add sugar and mix until it dissolves. Remove from heat and allow to cool a little. Add eggs and vanilla, beating well. Fold in the sifted flour.

Spread mixture into the tin, sprinkle with nuts and bake for about 12 minutes. Cool for 5 minutes, then cut into diamond shapes.

MAKES 36

Chocolate fruit slice

175 g dark chocolate (*not* cooking chocolate)

1 × 175-g packet mixed dried fruit

50 g glacé cherries

1 cup desiccated coconut

¼ cup castor sugar

2 tablespoons butter, melted

1 egg, beaten

Preheat oven to 180°C. Grease and line a 19-cm square cake tin.

Melt chocolate in a double boiler over simmering water, or on MEDIUM in the microwave, then spread it evenly over the base of the tin. Chill in the refrigerator until set.

Mix remaining ingredients together until well combined. Spread over chocolate base.

Bake for 20–25 minutes until golden brown.

Cool in the tin at room temperature, then chill at least 1 hour, until completely cold.

Cut into fingers and turn out of tin.

MAKES 36 | GLUTEN FREE

Chocolate fudge slice

180 g dark cooking chocolate, chopped

1 × 395-g tin condensed milk

2 teaspoons cocoa

1 teaspoon vanilla extract

300 g sweet gluten-free biscuits
  (such as sweet rice biscuits), crushed

⅓ cup slivered almonds or chopped nuts

1 cup mixed dried fruit

½ cup desiccated coconut

Grease and line a 19-cm × 29-cm slice tin.

Combine chocolate, condensed milk and sifted cocoa in a large microwave-safe bowl and microwave on MEDIUM for about 2 minutes, stirring occasionally, until chocolate has melted.

Add vanilla, biscuit crumbs, nuts and fruit to chocolate mixture and mix to combine.

Press mixture firmly into tin. Smooth the top and sprinkle with coconut. Cover and refrigerate until firm. Cut into bars to serve.

MAKES 36 | GLUTEN FREE | NO BAKE

Chocolate ginger rounds

1 cup gluten-free flour mix (page xiii)

2 tablespoons cocoa

25 g ground almonds

⅓ cup white sugar

1 egg, beaten

75 g butter, melted

2 tablespoons crystallised ginger, finely chopped

Preheat oven to 180°C. Lightly grease baking trays.

Sift together flour and cocoa. Add ground almonds and sugar and mix to combine. Add egg, butter and ginger and mix together until a soft dough forms.

Roll dough into walnut-sized balls and place on trays. Flatten slightly with a fork.

Bake for 12–15 minutes.

MAKES 36 | GLUTEN FREE

Chocolate jam slice

125 g softened butter

½ cup castor sugar

1 egg, beaten

½ teaspoon vanilla extract

2 cups self-raising flour

raspberry jam (or other fruit
   jam), for spreading

1 cup desiccated coconut

1 egg

½ cup white sugar

3 tablespoons cocoa

Preheat oven to 180°C. Lightly grease a 19-cm × 29-cm slice tin.

For the base, cream butter and sugar until light and fluffy. Beat in egg and vanilla extract. Add sifted flour and mix to a fairly stiff dough.

Press mixture into tin. Spread evenly with jam.

For coconut topping, beat all ingredients together. Spread over the jam.

Bake for 15–20 minutes. Cut into squares when cool.

MAKES 36

Chocolate molasses slice

1 cup plain flour

½ teaspoon baking powder

¼ teaspoon bicarbonate of soda

pinch of salt

1 cup walnuts, chopped

125 g butter

½ cup white sugar

½ cup molasses

1 egg

50 g cooking chocolate

Preheat oven to 180°C. Lightly grease a 19-cm × 29-cm slice tin.

Sift together flour, baking powder, bicarbonate of soda and salt. Mix in walnuts. In a separate bowl, cream the butter and sugar until light and creamy. Then beat in molasses and egg.

Melt chocolate in a double boiler over simmering water, or on MEDIUM in the microwave. Add melted chocolate to the creamed mixture and mix. Stir into the dry ingredients and mix well.

Pour into prepared tray and bake for 30 minutes or until firm. Cool in the tray for 5 minutes, then cut into squares and cool on a wire rack.

MAKES 24

Chocolate nut Florentines

1 cup soft brown sugar,
  lightly packed

125 g butter

½ cup golden syrup

1 cup self-raising flour

⅓ cup hazelnuts, chopped

⅓ cup blanched almonds,
  chopped

1 tablespoon mixed peel

1 tablespoon glacé cherries,
  chopped

125 g dark cooking chocolate

Preheat oven to 160°C. Line baking trays with baking paper.

Gently heat the sugar, butter and golden syrup in a saucepan until butter has melted and sugar has dissolved. Remove from heat and add sifted flour, nuts, peel and cherries. Mix thoroughly.

Drop spoonfuls of mixture onto the prepared trays, spaced well apart to allow for spreading. Bake for 12–15 minutes until lightly golden brown.

Cool on the trays for a few minutes before transferring to wire racks.

When the biscuits are cold, melt chocolate in a double boiler over simmering water, or on MEDIUM in the microwave. Spread melted chocolate over the flat side of each Florentine. (For a different look, dip one half of each biscuit in the melted chocolate.)

MAKES 18

Chocolate rice biscuits

100 g softened butter

½ cup castor sugar

1½ cups rice flour

2 tablespoons cocoa

1 egg, beaten

Preheat oven to 180°C. Lightly grease baking trays.

Cream butter and sugar until light and fluffy. Stir in sifted flour and cocoa. Add the egg and mix well to combine.

Roll mixture into small balls and place on baking trays. Flatten slightly with a fork. Bake for 12–18 minutes until brown.

VARIATIONS

For coffee biscuits, replace cocoa with 1 teaspoon instant coffee granules. For lemon or orange biscuits, replace cocoa with 1 tablespoon lemon or orange juice. For vanilla biscuits, replace the cocoa with ½ teaspoon vanilla extract.

MAKES 30 | GLUTEN FREE

Chocolate rocks

100 g dark cooking chocolate, chopped

80 g butter

1 cup plain flour

2 tablespoons cocoa

¼ teaspoon bicarbonate of soda

1 cup castor sugar

1 egg, beaten

icing sugar, for coating

Melt the chocolate and butter in a saucepan over low heat, or in the microwave on MEDIUM.

Sift together the flour, cocoa and bicarbonate of soda. Add to the chocolate mixture along with the sugar and egg. Mix well.

Chill in the refrigerator for at least 20 minutes.

Preheat oven to 180° C. Line baking trays with baking paper.

When dough is firm enough to handle, roll into small balls. Roll each ball in icing sugar, then place on the trays (leaving room for spreading). Bake for 15 minutes.

Cool on the trays before transferring to a wire rack.

MAKES 24

Cinnamon macaroons

2 cups white sugar

1 tablespoon ground cinnamon

7 egg whites

2 cups ground almonds

2 teaspoons finely grated lemon zest

2 cups castor sugar

Preheat oven to 160° C. Lightly grease and line baking trays.

Mix together white sugar and cinnamon.

In a separate bowl, beat egg whites until frothy. Add ¼ cup of the sugar mix at a time, beating all the while. Once all the sugar has been added, continue beating for about 10 minutes, until the mixture is very thick.

Fold ground almonds and lemon zest into the mixture, then fold in the castor sugar.

Drop spoonfuls of mixture onto prepared baking trays, leaving space for spreading. Bake for 25 minutes or until lightly browned.

MAKES 48 | GLUTEN FREE

Cinnamon mince slice

1 cup plain flour

½ cup rice flour

⅓ cup castor sugar

125 g cold butter, cut into
small pieces

2 eggs, separated

400 g fruit mince

2 tablespoons castor sugar mixed
with 1 teaspoon ground
cinnamon, for sprinkling

Preheat oven to 180°C. Grease and line a 20-cm × 30-cm lamington tin.

In a food processor, blend the sifted flours, sugar and butter until crumbly. With the motor running, add the egg yolks and blend until a soft dough forms.

Remove dough and knead gently on a lightly floured surface. Press two-thirds of the dough into the tin. Spread fruit mince evenly over the base and then crumble remaining dough over the top.

Beat egg whites until frothy and drizzle over the top. Sprinkle with the cinnamon sugar.

Bake for 20 minutes until golden brown. Cool before cutting into squares.

MAKES 24

Cinnamon orange squares

2 cups plain flour

1 teaspoon cinnamon

1 teaspoon bicarbonate of soda

grated zest and juice of 1 large
   orange

125 g butter

3 tablespoons orange marmalade

1/3 cup golden syrup

1/3 cup soft brown sugar

1/2 cup milk

1 egg, beaten

Preheat oven to 180°C. Grease and line a 19-cm × 29-cm slice tin.

Sift together flour, cinnamon and bicarbonate of soda. Then stir in orange zest.

In a saucepan, heat the butter, marmalade, golden syrup, sugar and milk until the butter melts. Add the orange juice.

Stir the liquid mixture into the dry ingredients, then add the egg and beat until smooth.

Pour into prepared tin and bake for 40 minutes. Cool in the tray, then transfer to a wire rack. Cut into squares when cold.

MAKES 20

Cinnamon sugar bars

2 tablespoons softened butter

⅔ cup castor sugar

1 cup self-raising flour

pinch of salt

1 teaspoon baking powder

1 teaspoon ground cinnamon

½ cup milk

1 egg, beaten

2 tablespoons castor sugar mixed
with 1 teaspoon ground
cinnamon, for sprinkling

Preheat oven to 180°C. Grease and line a 20-cm × 20-cm lamington tin.

Cream the butter and sugar until light and fluffy. In a separate bowl, sift together the flour, salt, baking powder and cinnamon. Mix into the creamed mixture. Mix the milk and egg together and beat into the mixture.

Spread into tin and bake for 15 minutes. Sprinkle generously with cinnamon sugar then return to the oven for another 10 minutes.

MAKES 18

Cocoa slice

1 cup self-raising flour

1 tablespoon cocoa

1 cup desiccated coconut

1 cup crushed Corn Flakes

½ cup white sugar

125 g butter, melted

chocolate glacé icing (page 241)

Preheat oven to 180°C. Lightly grease a 19-cm × 29-cm slice tin.

Sift together flour and cocoa. Stir in coconut, Corn Flakes and sugar. Mix in melted butter.

Press into tin and bake for 20–25 minutes.

While still hot, spread with chocolate icing and cut into squares. Remove from tin when cold.

MAKES 36

Coconut fancies

1¼ cups desiccated coconut

½ cup puffed rice cereal

1 × 395-g tin condensed milk

Preheat oven to 180°C. Grease and line baking trays.

Mix all ingredients together.

Spoon mixture onto trays. Cook for 25–30 minutes or until lightly browned.

Cool on the baking trays.

MAKES 24 | GLUTEN FREE

Coconut ice slice

BASE

115 g softened butter

¾ cup white sugar

1 egg, beaten

1 cup self-raising flour

¾ cup desiccated coconut

TOPPING

75 g butter, melted

3 cups icing sugar

1½ cups desiccated coconut

3 tablespoons milk

1½ teaspoons vanilla extract

Preheat oven to 180°C. Lightly grease a 19-cm × 29-cm slice tin.

For the base, cream the butter and sugar together until light and fluffy. Add egg, then sifted flour and coconut. Mix well.

Pour into tin and bake for 30 minutes.

For the topping, mix all ingredients together until well combined. Spread over the base while still hot. Cool, then cut into squares.

MAKES 36

Coconut rough slice

1 cup self-raising flour

3 teaspoons cocoa

pinch of salt

⅓ cup castor sugar

¼ cup desiccated coconut

115 g butter, melted

4 tablespoons condensed milk

1 tablespoon cocoa

1 cup icing sugar

30 g butter, melted

1 cup desiccated coconut

1 teaspoon vanilla extract

icing sugar, for dusting

Preheat oven to 160°C. Lightly grease a 19-cm × 29-cm slice tin.

For the base, sift together flour, cocoa and salt. Add sugar, coconut and melted butter and stir until well combined.

Press into prepared tin (it will be quite thin, as this slice rises during cooking). Bake for 25 minutes. Set aside to cool a little.

For the topping, mix all ingredients together until well combined. Spread over slice.

When cool, dust with icing sugar and cut into long fingers.

MAKES 24

Coffee layer slice

TOPPING

1 cup plain flour

1 teaspoon ground cinnamon

1 teaspoon mixed spice

⅓ cup soft brown sugar, firmly
    packed

125 g cold butter, cut into small
    pieces

BASE

125 g softened butter

¼ cup castor sugar

1 cup plain flour

¼ cup self-raising flour

FILLING

1 × 395-g tin condensed milk

30 g butter

2 tablespoons golden syrup

3 teaspoons instant coffee
    granules

⅓ cup finely chopped nuts
    (almonds, walnuts, etc.)

Preheat oven to 180°C. Lightly grease a 25-cm × 30-cm Swiss roll tin.

For the topping, sift together flour, spices and sugar. Rub in butter with your fingertips until crumbly. Mix into a firm dough. Refrigerate for 30 minutes while making the base.

For the base, cream butter and sugar until light and fluffy. Add sifted flours and mix to a firm dough. Press evenly over base of tin and bake for 15 minutes. Set aside to cool. (Leave oven on.) >

For the filling, combine condensed milk, butter, golden syrup and coffee in a saucepan. Stir over medium heat until it just begins to bubble, then cook for a further 3 minutes or until thick.

Remove from heat, stir in the nuts and spread over the base. Crumble or grate the chilled topping over the filling until evenly covered.

Bake for a further 20 minutes, or until the topping is firm. Cool in the tin for 15 minutes before cutting into squares. Leave in the tin to cool completely.

MAKES 40

Currant granola squares

3½ cups rolled oats

½ cup desiccated coconut

160 g butter, melted

4 tablespoons honey

1 egg, beaten

1 cup currants

1 cup nuts (e.g. walnuts,
  almonds, hazelnuts), chopped

½ cup soft brown sugar

½ teaspoon vanilla extract

pinch of salt

Preheat oven to 180°C. Grease a 25-cm × 30-cm Swiss roll tin.

Toast oats on a ungreased baking tray for about 20 minutes or until golden.

Combine oats with all other ingredients and mix well.

Press mixture firmly into tin. Bake for 20–25 minutes, until golden brown.
Cool before cutting into squares.

MAKES 36

Double dip Mars bar slice

BASE

4 × 65 g Mars bars

125 g butter

4 cups Rice Bubbles

TOPPING

200 g milk chocolate, chopped

30 g butter

Grease and line a 19-cm square cake tin.

For the base, melt together the Mars bars and butter in a heavy-bottomed saucepan over low heat. Add Rice Bubbles and mix well.

Press into tin. Refrigerate about 3 hours, until set.

For the topping, melt the chocolate and butter in a double boiler or heat on MEDIUM in the microwave, then stir until smooth. Spread over the base, leave to set, then cut into squares.

MAKES 24 | NO BAKE

Florentine bars

185 g dark cooking chocolate
¾ cup sultanas
2 cups Corn Flakes, crushed
½ cup mixed nuts, crushed
60 g glacé cherries, chopped
⅔ cup condensed milk

Grease and line a 19-cm × 29-cm slice tin.

Melt chocolate in a double boiler over simmering water, or on MEDIUM in the microwave.

Spread evenly over base of tin. Refrigerate until set.

Preheat oven to 180°C.

Combine sultanas, Corn Flakes, nuts, cherries and condensed milk in a bowl. Mix well.

Spread evenly over chocolate base. Bake for 15–20 minutes. Cool at room temperature, then chill until set before cutting into bars.

MAKES 36

Fresh berry slice

¼ cup softened butter

¾ cup white sugar

1 egg

2 cups self-raising flour

pinch of salt

raspberry jam, for spreading

½ cup fresh raspberries,
blueberries or blackberries

1 cup white sugar

1 cup desiccated coconut

1 egg

Preheat oven to 180°C. Lightly grease a 19-cm × 29-cm slice tin.

For the base, cream butter and sugar until light and fluffy. Mix in egg, sifted flour and salt.

Press mixture into tray, spread thickly with jam and sprinkle with fresh berries.

For the topping, mix all ingredients together and spread evenly over base.

Bake for about 20 minutes. Cool before slicing.

MAKES 24

Frilled Easter biscuits

115 g softened butter

⅓ cup castor sugar, plus extra
   for sprinkling

1 egg, separated

1¾ cups plain flour

½ teaspoon mixed spice

½ teaspoon ground cinnamon

⅓ cup currants

1 tablespoon mixed peel, finely
   chopped

1–2 tablespoons milk

Preheat oven to 180°C. Lightly grease baking trays.

Cream the butter and sugar until light and fluffy, then beat in the egg yolk.

Sift together flour and spices, then fold into the egg mixture. Stir in the currants and peel. Add enough milk to form a fairly soft dough.

Turn dough onto a lightly floured surface, knead gently, then roll out to 5 mm thick. Cut into rounds using a fluted biscuit cutter. Gather any leftover dough, roll out again and use to make more biscuits. Place on prepared trays and bake for 10 minutes.

Beat the egg white until frothy, then brush over the biscuits. Sprinkle with castor sugar and bake for another 10 minutes, or until golden.

MAKES 16

Fruity cereal bars

1 cup breakfast cereal with
dried fruit

1 cup self-raising wholemeal
flour

½ cup soft brown sugar

125 g butter, melted

1½ cups breakfast cereal with
dried fruit

2 eggs, beaten

1 teaspoon vanilla extract

¾ cup soft brown sugar

½ cup unsalted raw peanuts

Preheat oven to 180°C. Lightly grease a 19-cm × 29-cm slice tin.

For the base, mix all ingredients together until well combined.

Press mixture into tin and bake for 15 minutes.

For the topping, mix all ingredients together until well combined.
Spread over base.

Bake for a further 30–35 minutes. Cool in the tin before cutting
into slices.

MAKES 24

Fudgy fruit slice

¾ cup dates, chopped
¼ cup dried apricots, chopped
¼ cup preserved ginger, chopped
½ cup soft brown sugar
125 g butter
4 cups Rice Bubbles
desiccated coconut, for coating

Grease and line a 19-cm square cake tin.

In a heavy-bottomed saucepan, heat the dates, apricots, ginger, sugar and butter. Simmer about 15 minutes, until the fruit is soft and fudgy. (Do not cook for too long, as the mixture may burn or start to set.)

Add Rice Bubbles and mix well. Press into tin. Set in the refrigerator for at least 2 hours, then cut into cubes and coat in coconut.

MAKES 16 | NO BAKE

Georgian baklava

PASTRY

250 g cold butter, cut into small
    pieces

1¾ cups plain flour

½ teaspoon bicarbonate of soda

1 egg yolk

1 cup sour cream

FILLING

½ cup walnuts, finely ground

1 cup white sugar

½ teaspoon vanilla extract

2 egg whites

1 egg yolk, beaten

For the pastry, blend the butter with the flour and bicarbonate of soda in
a food processor until crumbly. Add the egg yolk and sour cream and blend
to make a soft dough. Wrap dough in plastic film and refrigerate for at least
2 hours.

Preheat oven to 180°C. Lightly grease a 19-cm square cake tin and dust
with flour.

For the filling, combine the ground walnuts with the sugar and vanilla.
In a separate bowl beat the egg whites until stiff peaks form. Gently fold
egg whites into the nut mixture.

Divide the dough into three pieces, and roll each out to the size of the tin.
Use the first pastry sheet to line the base of the tin. Spread with half the
filling, leaving a 2-cm border all the way around. Place the second sheet
on top.

Cover with the remaining filling and top with the last piece of dough. Tuck the edges of the dough under to seal. Press down firmly with your hands.

Score the top of the slice into diamonds, using a sharp knife. Brush with egg yolk.

Bake for 45–50 minutes or until golden brown. Cut into diamonds to serve.

MAKES 48

Ginger and date slice

1 cup dates, chopped

250 g butter

⅓ cup castor sugar

60 g preserved ginger, finely chopped

3 cups Corn Flakes

125 g dark cooking chocolate, chopped

Grease and line a 19-cm × 29-cm slice tin.

Combine dates, butter, sugar and ginger in a saucepan and stir over low heat until well mixed and mushy. Add Corn Flakes and mix well.

Press mixture into tin and refrigerate until cold and firm.

Melt chocolate in a double boiler over simmering water, or on MEDIUM in the microwave, then spread over slice. Chill for about 5 minutes to allow the chocolate to set a little, then mark out squares by scoring lines in the top with a sharp knife.

Return to refrigerator and chill until completely set. Cut into squares along the scored lines.

MAKES 36 | NO BAKE

Ginger biscuits

1¼ cup gluten-free flour mix
   (page xiii)

1½ teaspoons bicarbonate of
   soda

½ teaspoon cream of tartar

2 teaspoons ground ginger

½ cup white sugar

¼ cup olive oil

2 tablespoons golden syrup

1 egg, beaten

Preheat oven to 190°C. Lightly grease trays.

Sift together flour, bicarbonate of soda, cream of tartar and ginger. Stir in sugar. Warm the oil and golden syrup together until blended. Allow to cool slightly, then add to the dry ingredients. Add the beaten egg and mix until a firm dough forms.

Roll dough into walnut-sized balls and place on trays, leaving plenty of space for spreading.

Bake for 15–20 minutes or until brown.

VARIATION

For gluten-free gingerbread men substitute treacle for the golden syrup and reduce bicarbonate of soda to ½ teaspoon. Roll out the dough to 5 mm thick or less, then cut out gingerbread men shapes with a biscuit cutter.

MAKES 36 | GLUTEN FREE

Gingerbread men

125 g butter

2 tablespoons golden syrup

¾ cup white sugar

1 egg, beaten

2 cups self-raising flour

pinch of salt

2 teaspoons ground ginger

currants, cherries, liquorice, chocolate chips, etc., for decorating

Preheat oven to 150°C. Lightly grease baking trays.

Melt butter and golden syrup over low heat, then remove from heat and stir in sugar and egg.

Add the sifted flour, salt and ginger and mix well.

Turn dough onto a lightly floured surface, and knead gently until the dough forms a ball. Roll out thinly. Use biscuit cutters to cut out gingerbread men (or other shapes). Gather any leftover dough, roll out again and use to make more biscuits.

Place on trays and add dried fruit, chocolate and lollies to make eyes, mouth, buttons, etc. Bake for about 10 minutes, until golden brown.

MAKES 18

Gingerbread squares

3 cups plain flour

1 teaspoon bicarbonate of soda

3 teaspoons ground ginger

pinch of salt

2 tablespoons cold butter, cut
    into small pieces

2 tablespoons soft brown sugar

¾ cup golden syrup

1 egg, beaten

1 cup milk

lemon glacé icing (page 241)

Preheat oven to 180°C. Lightly grease a 20-cm × 30-cm lamington tin.

Sift together the flour, bicarbonate of soda, ginger and salt. Rub in the butter with your fingertips until crumbly, then mix in sugar.

Heat golden syrup until just warm, then mix with egg and milk. Add to the dry ingredients and mix until smooth.

Pour into prepared tin and bake for 30–35 minutes or until risen and set.

Once cool, top with lemon icing. Cut into squares to serve.

MAKES 24

Ginger crunch

125 g softened butter

½ cup white sugar

2 cups plain flour

1 teaspoon baking powder

1 teaspoon ground ginger

80 g butter

½ cup icing sugar

1 tablespoon golden syrup

2 teaspoons ground ginger

Preheat oven to 180°C. Lightly grease a 23-cm square slab tin.

For the base, cream butter and sugar until light and fluffy. In a separate bowl sift together flour, baking powder and ginger. Fold into creamed mixture to form a dough.

Turn onto a lightly floured surface and knead dough well. Press into prepared tin.

Bake 20–25 minutes or until firm to touch and lightly golden brown.

For the topping, heat all ingredients in a saucepan until smooth. Pour over slice while still hot. Cool for 5 minutes before cutting into squares.

MAKES 24

Ginger nuts

125 g butter

1 cup white sugar

1 tablespoon golden syrup

1 egg, beaten

2 cups self-raising flour

½ teaspoon bicarbonate of soda

2 teaspoons ground ginger

1 teaspoon mixed spice

Preheat oven to 220°C. Lightly grease baking trays.

Gently heat butter, sugar and golden syrup until butter has melted and sugar has dissolved. Remove from heat, cool slightly, then add egg.

Add sifted dry ingredients and mix thoroughly.

Roll dough into walnut-sized balls. Place on baking trays, leaving space for spreading. Chill for 15 minutes.

Bake for 5 minutes, then reduce heat to 180°C and bake for a further 7–10 minutes.

Cool on trays until nearly cold before transferring to wire racks to cool completely.

MAKES 36

Ginger sticks

4 eggs, separated

⅓ cup castor sugar, plus extra
    for sprinkling

1 tablespoon ground ginger

1⅔ cups gluten-free flour mix (page xiii)

icing sugar, for dusting

Preheat oven to 180°C. Lightly grease baking trays.

Mix the egg yolks with the sugar and ginger to form a smooth paste.
Beat egg whites until stiff peaks form. Fold a spoonful into the egg-yolk
mixture, then gently fold in remaining egg white, alternately with the flour.

Put mixture into a piping bag and pipe 5-cm long sticks onto the prepared
baking trays.

Sprinkle with castor sugar and bake for 8–10 minutes or until light brown.

Dust with icing sugar to serve.

MAKES 30 | GLUTEN FREE

Glazed lemon jumbles

2¾ cups plain flour

1 teaspoon cream of tartar

½ teaspoon bicarbonate of soda

pinch of salt

250 g softened butter

1 cup white sugar

1 egg

1 tablespoon finely grated
  lemon zest

1 tablespoon lemon juice

1 teaspoon almond essence

GLAZE

2 cups icing sugar

2 tablespoons butter, melted

3 tablespoons lemon juice

yellow food colouring (optional)

Preheat oven to 180°C. Lightly grease baking trays.

Sift together the flour, cream of tartar, bicarbonate of soda and salt.

In a separate bowl, cream the butter, sugar, egg, lemon zest, lemon juice and almond essence until light and well blended.

Stir in the flour mixture and combine well.

Shape the dough into a ball, divide into four pieces, then roll out each piece into a flat round. Cut each round into 12 wedges.

Roll each wedge into a 10-cm long rope, of even width. Bring the ends together and press firmly to create a ring.

Place rings on baking trays, leaving space between for spreading.

Bake for 8–12 minutes or until slightly golden at the edges. Transfer immediately to a wire rack to cool.

To make the glaze, beat together all ingredients until smooth. If necessary, add extra lemon juice to produce a thin glaze.

Dip the top of each ring into the glaze and shake off excess. Let stand 1 hour or until glaze is completely set. If desired, add a little yellow food colouring to any leftover icing, then pipe or drizzle zigzag lines across the glazed areas.

MAKES 48

Golden slice

BASE

125 g softened butter

½ cup white sugar

1 teaspoon vanilla extract

1 cup plain flour

1 cup desiccated coconut

FILLING

1 × 395-g tin condensed milk

60 g butter

2 tablespoons golden syrup

TOPPING

60 g butter

1 tablespoon golden syrup

1 cup desiccated coconut

½ cup sweet biscuit crumbs
  or rolled oats

Preheat oven to 180°C. Lightly grease a 20-cm × 30-cm lamington tin.

For the base, cream butter, sugar and vanilla until light and creamy. Add sifted flour and coconut. Mix well.

Press mixture evenly into tin. Bake for 20 minutes, then remove and cool slightly. (Leave oven on.)

Meanwhile, make the caramel filling by combining all ingredients in a saucepan and stirring over a low heat until the butter melts. Turn up heat slightly and simmer gently for about 5 minutes, stirring continuously. Remove from the heat as soon as it reaches a light caramel colour. Spread over the base.

For the topping, stir butter and golden syrup in a saucepan over low heat until the butter has melted. Add the coconut and biscuit crumbs or oats and mix well. Sprinkle topping evenly over filling.

Return to oven and bake another 15–20 minutes or until golden brown. Cool before cutting into slices.

MAKES 36

Ham and cheese slice

BASE

2 cups self-raising flour

½ teaspoon salt

75 g cold butter, cut into pieces

½ cup milk

¼ cup mayonnaise

FILLING

2 tablespoons Dijon or
wholegrain mustard

225 g ham, shredded

1 cup chopped onion

125 g grated tasty cheese,
plus extra for sprinkling

salt and freshly ground
black pepper

2 tablespoons chopped fresh
parsley

milk, for brushing

Preheat oven to 220°C. Lightly grease a 20-cm × 30-cm lamington tin.

For the base, sift together flour and salt, then rub in butter with your fingertips until crumbly. Combine milk and mayonnaise and add to the dry ingredients, mixing until a soft dough forms.

Divide dough in half. Roll out the first portion on a lightly floured surface to fit the base of the prepared tin.

For the filling, spread mustard thinly over the base and sprinkle over the ham. In a bowl, combine the onion, cheese, salt and pepper and parsley. Spread evenly over the ham.

Roll out remaining pastry and use to cover the filling. Brush top with milk and sprinkle with extra cheese.

Bake for 20 minutes. Cut into squares while still warm.

MAKES 16

Hazelnut crescents

250 g softened butter

½ cup icing sugar, plus extra
   for dusting

1 teaspoon vanilla extract

1 egg yolk

2½ cups self-raising flour

¾ cup ground hazelnuts

Preheat oven to 180°C. Line baking trays with baking paper.

Cream butter and sifted icing sugar until light and fluffy. Add vanilla and egg yolk and beat until well combined.

Fold in sifted flour and ground hazelnuts until just combined. If the dough is too firm, add two teaspoons of iced water.

Take tablespoons of the dough and shape into 8-cm crescents. Place crescents 2 cm apart on prepared trays.

Cook for about 12 minutes, or until lightly browned. Allow crescents to cool on trays. Serve heavily dusted with icing sugar.

MAKES 36

Health biscuits

125 g softened butter

¼ cup castor sugar

2 tablespoons honey

1 egg

1 cup wholemeal flour

½ cup self-raising flour

½ cup plain flour

¼ cup bran, plus extra
    for sprinkling

pinch of salt

Preheat oven to 180°C. Lightly grease baking trays.

Cream butter and sugar until very light and creamy. Add honey and egg and beat until well combined.

Add sifted flours, bran and salt and mix well.

Turn dough onto lightly floured surface and knead gently. Roll dough out to 3 mm in thickness and sprinkle with a little extra bran. Run a rolling pin lightly over it to press the bran into the dough.

Using a 6-cm biscuit cutter, cut pastry into rounds. Place rounds on baking trays. Prick biscuit all over with a fork.

Bake for 12–15 minutes or until light golden brown. Cool for 5 minutes on the tray before transferring to wire racks.

MAKES 24

Herby cheese crackers

¾ cup softened butter

½ cup grated cheddar cheese

⅓ cup crumbled blue cheese

1 cup wholemeal flour

1 small clove garlic, crushed

1 teaspoon finely chopped fresh parsley

1 teaspoon finely chopped fresh chives

1 teaspoon finely chopped fresh oregano

Cream butter and cheeses until smooth. Add sifted flour, garlic and herbs and mix well. If necessary, add a little cold water to make the dough hold together.

Roll dough into a log 4-cm in diameter and chill for at least 30 minutes.

Preheat oven to 190°C. Lightly grease baking trays.

Slice dough into rounds and place on baking trays. Bake for 8–10 minutes.

MAKES 40

Hodge podge

125 g butter

½ cup white sugar

1 tablespoon golden syrup

1 egg, lightly beaten

1½ cups plain flour

½ cup self-raising flour

1 teaspoon nutmeg

2 cups mixed dried fruit

¼ cup raw almonds, coarsely chopped

Preheat oven to 170°C. Grease and line a deep 19-cm × 29-cm slice tin.

Heat butter, sugar and golden syrup in a saucepan until butter has melted and sugar has almost dissolved. Remove from heat and cool for a few minutes so egg doesn't scramble when added. Mix in egg.

Sift together flours and nutmeg, then stir in fruit and nuts. Mix in the liquid mixture.

Press into the slice tin. Bake for about 30 minutes or until a skewer inserted into the centre comes out clean and the slice is nicely browned.

MAKES 20

Homemade mint slice

1½ cups self-raising flour

½ cup soft brown sugar

1 cup desiccated coconut

180 g butter, melted

1¼ cups icing sugar

1½ tablespoons milk

1 tablespoon white vegetable shortening, melted

1 teaspoon peppermint essence

½ cup drinking chocolate powder

3 tablespoons white vegetable shortening, melted

Preheat oven to 180°C. Lightly grease a 19-cm × 29-cm slice tin.

For the base, mix together sifted flour, sugar and coconut. Stir in melted butter.

Press into the tin and bake for 15–20 minutes, or until golden.

For the filling, mix together sifted icing sugar, milk, shortening and peppermint. Pour over the warm base. Leave to set.

For the topping, mix drinking chocolate and shortening to a smooth paste. When filling has set, spread with icing. Let icing set before cutting into small squares.

MAKES 36

Homemade water crackers

1 cup plain flour

½ teaspoon baking powder

pinch of salt

30 g cold butter, cut into small pieces

sea salt, for sprinkling

Preheat oven to 200°C. Lightly grease baking trays.

Sift together flour, baking powder and salt. Rub butter into the flour with your fingertips until crumbly. Stir in just enough water to bring the ingredients together into a firm dough.

Roll out dough to about 5 mm in thickness. Cut into small rounds with a biscuit cutter. Gather any leftover dough, roll out again and use to make more biscuits.

Take the rounds and roll out again until they are very thin and oval in shape. Place on baking trays and lightly prick all over with a fork.

Brush crackers with water and sprinkle with sea salt.

Bake for 10 minutes until golden and slightly puffed.

VARIATIONS

Substitute the sea salt with freshly ground black pepper, sesame seeds, mixed dried herbs or cumin seeds.

MAKES 30

Honeybunch hearts

185 g softened butter

½ cup castor sugar

6 tablespoons honey

1 egg

2½ cups plain flour

½ teaspoon mixed spice

½ teaspoon ground cinnamon

100 g dark cooking chocolate, chopped

In a food processor, blend the butter, sugar and honey until smooth. Add the egg and blend until combined.

Add sifted flour and spices and process until a smooth dough forms. Wrap dough in plastic film and chill in the refrigerator for 30 minutes.

Preheat oven to 180°C. Line baking trays with baking paper.

Roll out dough between 2 sheets of non-stick baking paper until 3 mm thick. Using a heart-shaped biscuit cutter, cut out biscuits. Gather any leftover dough, roll out again and use to make more biscuits.

Place hearts on the prepared trays and cook for 12–15 minutes, or until golden and crisp. Cool on a wire rack.

When the biscuits are cold, melt chocolate in a double boiler over simmering water, or on MEDIUM in the microwave. Dip one half of each biscuit in the melted chocolate.

MAKES 16

Honey joys

2 tablespoons butter

2 tablespoons castor sugar

1 tablespoon honey

5 cups Corn Flakes

Preheat oven to 150°C.

Melt butter, sugar and honey over low heat. Remove from heat and mix in Corn Flakes.

Place spoonfuls into paper patty cases and bake for about 20 minutes. Set aside until cool and set.

MAKES 36

Jamaica slice

25 g butter, cut into small pieces

200 g dark cooking chocolate, chopped

½ cup castor sugar

1 cup raisins, chopped

2 eggs, lightly beaten

1½ cups plain flour

1 tablespoon rum

icing sugar or cocoa, for dusting

Preheat oven to 160°C. Lightly grease a 20-cm × 30-cm lamington tin.

Combine butter, chocolate, sugar and raisins in a saucepan and heat gently until the chocolate has melted. Remove from heat and cool for a few minutes so eggs don't scramble when added. Stir in eggs, sifted flour and rum and mix well.

Spread mixture into the prepared tray and bake for about 30 minutes, or until just firm to the touch.

Cool in the tray, dust with icing sugar or cocoa and cut into slices.

MAKES 40

Jam bars

185 g softened butter

1 egg

1 teaspoon vanilla extract

2 cups plain flour

½ teaspoon baking powder

⅔ cup castor sugar

raspberry or apricot jam (or other fruit jam), for filling

Preheat oven to 180°C.

Cream butter until fluffy, then beat in egg and vanilla.

Stir in sifted flour, baking powder and sugar, to form a dough.

Turn on to a lightly floured surface. Divide into four pieces and shape each into a roll about 2-cm in diameter.

Arrange on ungreased baking trays, about 10 cm apart. Using a knife handle, make a depression about 5-mm deep lengthwise along the centre of each roll. Fill with jam.

Bake for 15–20 minutes.

Remove from the oven and cut each roll diagonally into bars while still warm. Transfer to a wire rack to cool.

MAKES 24

Jam fancies

1 cup plain flour

pinch of salt

½ cup castor sugar

125 g butter, cut into
    small pieces

125 g cream cheese, cut into
    small pieces

raspberry jam, for spreading

Sift flour and salt together, then mix in sugar. Add butter and cream cheese and blend thoroughly to form a very soft dough.

Shape dough into a ball, wrap in plastic film and refrigerate for 1 hour.

Preheat oven to 200°C. Lightly grease baking trays and dust with flour.

Roll dough out to 3-mm in thickness and cut into circles with a 5-cm biscuit cutter. Remove the centres from half the rounds using a 2.5-cm cutter. Gather any leftover dough, roll out again and use to make more rounds and rings.

Place biscuits on baking trays, leaving space for spreading. Bake for 10–12 minutes, or until golden brown.

When cool, spread rounds with raspberry jam and place a ring on top.

MAKES 36

Jennifer's flapjacks

1 cup soft brown sugar

170 g butter

1 dessertspoon golden syrup

2 cups rolled oats

Preheat oven to 170°C. Lightly grease a 19-cm × 29-cm slice tin.

Combine the sugar, butter and golden syrup in a saucepan over medium heat. Stir until butter has melted and sugar has dissolved, then mix in the oats.

Press into the tin and bake for about 20 minutes or until golden brown. Cool before cutting into thick slices.

MAKES 16

Kiss cakes

125 g softened butter
1 cup castor sugar
2 eggs
1 cup self-raising flour
1 cup cornflour
raspberry jam, for spreading
icing sugar, for dusting

Preheat oven to 190°C. Lightly grease baking trays.

Cream butter and sugar until light and fluffy. Beat in eggs one at a time. Mix in sifted flour and cornflour.

Drop teaspoonfuls onto prepared trays and bake for 8–10 minutes, or until pale golden brown.

When cold, sandwich together with raspberry jam and dust generously with icing sugar.

MAKES 24

Kiwi chocolate-iced slice

BASE

1 cup plain flour

1 teaspoon baking powder

2 tablespoons cocoa

½ cup white sugar

¾ cup desiccated coconut

125 g butter, melted

TOPPING

1 cup icing sugar

2 teaspoons cocoa

¾ cup desiccated coconut,
plus extra for sprinkling

2 tablespoons butter, melted

¼ teaspoon vanilla extract

Preheat oven to 180°C. Lightly grease a 19-cm × 29-cm slice tin.

For the base, sift together flour, baking powder and cocoa, then mix in sugar and coconut. Stir in melted butter and mix until well combined.

Press mixture into tin. Bake for about 15 minutes.

For the topping, sift together sugar and cocoa, then stir in coconut. Mix to a paste with butter and vanilla.

When slice is cool, ice with topping and sprinkle with extra coconut.

MAKES 24

Korzhiki (Russian shortbread)

2 cups plain flour

pinch of salt

½ teaspoon baking powder

½ cup sour cream

2 eggs

3 tablespoons castor sugar

2 tablespoons softened butter, diced

Preheat oven to 220° C. Lightly grease baking trays.

Sift together the flour, salt and baking powder. Make a well in the centre, add the sour cream, 1 egg, sugar and butter, and stir until a moist dough forms.

Roll out on a lightly floured surface until about 5 mm thick. Cut into rounds using a biscuit cutter, then prick all over with a fork and brush with the remaining egg.

Bake for 10–15 minutes or until lightly browned.

MAKES 36

Lebkuchen

1 cup castor sugar

2 eggs

¾ tablespoon finely grated
lemon zest

2 cups ground almonds

⅓ cup mixed peel, finely
chopped

½ teaspoon ground nutmeg

½ teaspoon ground cinnamon

½ teaspoon ground cloves

½ teaspoon ground cardamom

ICING

1 cup icing sugar

2 tablespoons lemon juice

Preheat oven to 180° C. Lightly grease baking trays.

Cream sugar, eggs and zest until very light and fluffy. Add remaining
ingredients and mix to a firm dough.

Drop dessertspoonfuls of mixture onto prepared trays, leaving about
5 cm between biscuits for spreading. Bake for 10 minutes or until golden.

To make the icing, beat the sifted icing sugar and lemon juice until smooth
(add a little more or a little less lemon juice to create the consistency you
desire). When the biscuits are cold, spread on the icing.

MAKES 40 | GLUTEN FREE

Lemon fluff slice

BASE

1 cup plain flour

1 cup self-raising flour

125 g cold butter, cut into small
pieces

½ cup white sugar

½ teaspoon vanilla extract

1 egg, beaten

FILLING

1½ cups white sugar

2 cups water

finely grated zest and juice
of 2 lemons

¼ cup custard powder

¼ cup cornflour

2 tablespoons butter, melted

TOPPING

1 cup white sugar

1 cup water

2 dessertspoons gelatine

pinch of cream of tartar

desiccated coconut, for
sprinkling

Preheat oven to 180°C. Lightly grease a 19-cm × 29-cm slice tin.

For the base, sift flours together, then rub in butter using your fingertips
until crumbly. Add sugar and vanilla, then mix to a dough with the egg.

Press mixture into tin and bake until golden. Cool.

For the lemon filling, place sugar, water, lemon juice and zest in a saucepan.
Bring to the boil.

In a small bowl or cup, blend sifted custard powder and cornflour to a paste with a little cold water. Stir into the lemon mixture to thicken, then add butter and mix well. Pour filling over cooked biscuit base and leave to cool.

For the marshmallow topping, bring sugar, water and gelatine to the boil in a saucepan. Add cream of tartar and simmer for 8 minutes. Allow to cool, then beat until thick and fluffy.

Pour topping over lemon filling. Toast coconut in a dry frying pan, then sprinkle over slice. Cut into slices when completely set.

MAKES 36

Lemon jelly layer squares

BASE

180 g butter, melted

250 g sweet biscuits, crushed

FILLING

1 × 395-g tin condensed milk

½ cup lemon juice

2 teaspoons gelatine

¾ cup boiling water

TOPPING

1 teaspoon gelatine

1 packet lemon-flavoured
    jelly crystals

1 cup boiling water

Lightly grease a 20-cm × 30-cm lamington tin.

For the base, mix butter and biscuits together, then press evenly into tin.
Chill until cold.

For the lemon filling, mix condensed milk with lemon juice. Dissolve gelatine
in boiling water, cool, then stir into condensed milk mixture. Spread filling
over the biscuit base. Chill again until cold.

For the topping, dissolve gelatine and jelly crystals in boiling water, then set
aside to cool. When slightly gluggy (a bit like egg whites), pour over the slice.
Return to the refrigerator and chill until jelly topping has set completely, then
cut into squares.

MAKES 24

Lemon sponge biscuits

3 eggs, separated
⅓ cup white sugar, plus extra for dusting
3 tablespoons ground almonds
⅓ cup rice flour
2 tablespoons potato flour
finely grated zest of 1 lemon

Preheat oven to 160°C. Grease and line baking trays.

Beat egg yolks with sugar to form a stiff paste. Mix in the ground almonds, sifted flours and lemon zest.

In a separate bowl, beat egg whites until stiff peaks form, then gently fold into the almond mixture.

Drop spoonfuls of mixture onto prepared trays and dust with sugar.

Bake for 8–10 minutes. Turn out onto a wire rack and return to the oven, at its very lowest setting, for 1 hour.

MAKES 36 | GLUTEN FREE

Lucy's ginger slice

1 cup self-raising flour

1 cup desiccated coconut

¾ cup white sugar

1 cup mixed dried fruit

¼ cup preserved ginger, finely chopped

250 g butter, melted

1 egg, lightly beaten

¼ teaspoon vanilla extract

sesame seeds or desiccated coconut, for sprinkling

Preheat oven to 180°C. Lightly grease a 19-cm × 29-cm slice tin.

Mix together sifted flour, coconut, sugar, dried fruit and ginger. Add butter, egg and vanilla and mix well.

Press mixture into tin and sprinkle top with sesame seeds or coconut. Bake for 20 minutes. Cool completely before cutting into slices.

MAKES 24

Macadamia meringue squares

100 g softened butter

½ cup castor sugar

2 eggs

½ teaspoon vanilla extract

1½ cups plain flour

pinch of salt

1 teaspoon baking powder

100 g macadamia nuts, chopped

¾ cup soft brown sugar

Preheat oven to 180° C. Lightly grease a 19-cm × 29-cm slice tin.

Cream butter and castor sugar until light and fluffy. Separate the eggs, keeping the two whites separate. In a small bowl, beat the egg yolks and 1 egg white. Add to the creamed mixture, along with the vanilla, and beat well.

Mix in sifted flour, salt and baking powder.

Press into the tin and sprinkle with the nuts.

Beat the remaining egg white until stiff peaks form, then fold in sifted soft brown sugar. Spread meringue over the top of the slice and bake for 20–25 minutes. When cool, cut into squares.

MAKES 24

Maraschino marshmallow slice

½ cup chopped almonds

1 cup desiccated coconut

75 g butter

250 g pink marshmallows

¾ cup sultanas

¼ cup maraschino cherries, drained and halved

4 cups Corn Flakes

125 g dark cooking chocolate, chopped

Lightly grease a 19-cm × 29-cm slice tin.

In a dry frying pan, lightly toast the almonds and coconut until golden.

Melt the butter and marshmallows over a low heat. Mix in toasted almonds and coconut, sultanas, cherries and Corn Flakes.

Press mixture into prepared tin and chill until set.

Melt chocolate in a double boiler over simmering water, or on MEDIUM in the microwave, then spread over slice. Cut into small squares when set.

MAKES 36 | NO BAKE

Maria's easy-peasy biscuits

2½ cups self-raising flour
¾ cup white sugar
1 tablespoon berry jam (or other fruit jam)
250 g butter, melted

Preheat oven to 180°C. Lightly grease baking trays.

Combine sifted flour, sugar and jam in a bowl. Mix in melted butter.

Place teaspoonfuls of mixture onto the prepared trays, leaving plenty of space between each for spreading.

Bake for 12–15 minutes or until lightly coloured.

MAKES 30

Marshmallow fingers

1 cup self-raising flour

1 dessertspoon cocoa

3 Weet-Bix biscuits, crushed

½ cup white sugar

½ cup desiccated coconut

115 g butter, melted

1 cup white sugar

1 dessertspoon gelatine

¾ cup water

few drops food colouring
(optional)

Preheat oven to 180°C. Lightly grease a 19-cm × 29-cm slice tin.

For the base, sift together flour and cocoa, then stir in Weet-Bix, sugar and coconut. Add butter and mix until well combined.

Press into the tin. Bake for 12–15 minutes.

For the marshmallow topping, combine all ingredients (except colouring) in a saucepan and boil for 3 minutes. Cool, then add food colouring (if using). Beat until very thick, then spread over slice. Slice into fingers once set.

MAKES 16

Marzipan marvels

240 g butter

1 cup soft brown sugar

1 egg

2½ cups plain flour

4 tablespoons cocoa

200 g marzipan

115 g white cooking chocolate, chopped

Preheat oven to 180°C. Lightly grease baking trays.

Cream the butter and sugar until light and fluffy. Add the egg and beat well.

Stir in the sifted flour and cocoa, then knead with your hands to form a soft dough.

On a lightly floured surface, roll dough out to 5 mm thickness. Cut into rounds using a 5-cm biscuit cutter. Gather any leftover dough, roll out again and cut more rounds, until you have 72 in total.

Roll marzipan into 36 small balls. Place half the biscuit rounds on the prepared trays, place a marzipan ball in the centre of each, then top each with a second biscuit round. Use a fork to press around the edges to seal. Bake for 10–12 minutes until well-risen.

When the biscuits are cold, melt white chocolate in a double boiler or on MEDIUM in the microwave. Drizzle melted chocolate over each biscuit.

MAKES 36

Meringues

2 egg whites

5 tablespoons castor sugar

Preheat oven to 120°C. Grease and line a large baking tray.

Beat egg whites until stiff peaks form. Gradually add sugar until stiff glossy peaks form.

Drop dessertspoonfuls of mixture onto prepared tray.

Bake for 1–1½ hours or until crisp and firm, but not browned.

Serve plain or sandwiched together with whipped cream.

VARIATIONS

Add 2 teaspoons instant coffee granules or a few drops food colouring or flavoured essence with the sugar.

MAKES 16 | GLUTEN FREE

Mince slice

BASE

2 cups self-raising flour

pinch of salt

125 g cold butter, cut into small
    pieces

1 teaspoon white sugar

FILLING

1 cup sultanas

1 cup currants

½ cup nuts

castor sugar, for sprinkling

icing sugar, for dusting

Preheat oven to 180°C. Lightly grease a 19-cm × 29-cm slice tin.

For the base, sift flour and salt, then rub in butter with your fingertips until crumbly. Add sugar, then mix in enough cold water to make a stiff dough.

Knead gently on a lightly floured surface.

For the filling, finely mince the fruit and nuts in a food processor. Sprinkle with a little castor sugar, to taste.

Divide dough into two pieces and roll each out thinly. Use the first sheet to line the base and sides of the tin. Spread over the minced fruit mixture, then cover with the second sheet of dough. Press dough together to seal, then score squares in the top with a sharp knife.

Bake for 10–15 minutes. Dust with icing sugar just before serving.

MAKES 36

Mocha creams

200 g softened unsalted butter

½ cup icing sugar

½ cup cornflour

1 cup plain flour

¼ cup cocoa, plus extra for dusting

400 g milk chocolate, chopped

100 g softened unsalted butter

1 cup icing sugar

2 teaspoons instant coffee granules

2 teaspoons hot water

Preheat oven to 180°C. Line baking trays with baking paper.

Cream butter and icing sugar until light and creamy. Sift together flours and cocoa and fold into creamed mixture until combined.

Roll dessertspoonfuls of mixture into balls. Place balls 2-cm apart on prepared trays and flatten slightly with the back of a spoon.

Bake for 8 minutes, or until lightly browned. Cool on trays for 5 minutes, then transfer to a wire rack.

Melt chocolate in a double boiler over simmering water, or on MEDIUM in the microwave.

Once biscuits are cool, use a fork to dip them into the melted chocolate. Place biscuits on a tray lined with baking paper and refrigerate until the chocolate is set.

To make the mocha cream, cream butter until light and fluffy. Gradually beat in sifted icing sugar until combined. Dissolve coffee in hot water and add to mixture, beating until just combined.

Spoon mocha cream into a piping bag fitted with a 1.5-cm fluted nozzle and pipe small rosettes onto each biscuit. (If you don't have a piping bag, you can just spread it on with a spatula.) Refrigerate biscuits until ready to eat.

Dust with a little cocoa just before serving.

MAKES 40

Mrs Baillie's sunflower and honey squares

125 g butter
¾ cup honey
4½ cups Corn Flakes, crushed
⅔ cup sunflower seeds (kernels)
⅓ cup desiccated coconut
⅓ cup glacé cherries

Lightly grease a 19-cm × 29-cm slice tin.

Melt butter and honey in a saucepan and simmer for 5 minutes.

Combine Corn Flakes, sunflower seeds, coconut and cherries in a large bowl. Pour the liquid over and mix well to combine.

Press into tin and refrigerate until set. Cut into squares when cold.

MAKES 16 | NO BAKE

Mum's chocolate walnut slice

125 g butter
½ cup white sugar
2 tablespoons cocoa
1 egg, beaten
250 g plain sweet biscuits, crushed
¾ cup walnuts, chopped

Lightly grease a 19-cm × 29-cm slice tin.

Stir butter and sugar in a saucepan over medium heat until butter has melted and sugar dissolved. Add sifted cocoa and egg and bring to the boil, stirring continuously.

Add crushed biscuits and nuts, and mix until well combined.

Press into tin and refrigerate until set. Top with icing when cold if desired (see pages 241–44).

MAKES 36 | NO BAKE

Nanna Molly's melting moments

250 g softened unsalted butter

4 tablespoons icing sugar

4 tablespoons cornflour

1½ cups plain flour

1½ cups icing sugar

2 tablespoons softened butter

1 tablespoon vanilla extract
(or lemon juice or
passionfruit pulp)

Preheat oven to 160°C. Line baking trays with baking paper.

Cream butter and sugar until light and fluffy. Gradually beat in sifted flour and cornflour.

Roll heaped teaspoonfuls of mixture into balls and place on baking tray, flattening each slightly with a fork.

Bake for 15–20 minutes until firm and golden. (Be careful not to burn them.)

For the filling, beat sifted icing sugar and butter together until creamy. Mix in vanilla extract (or lemon juice or passionfruit pulp). Once biscuits are cold, sandwich together with filling.

MAKES 32

Nutmeg cannonballs

250 g softened butter

$\frac{1}{2}$ cup white sugar

2 teaspoons vanilla extract

2 cups plain flour

$1\frac{1}{2}$ cups ground almonds

$\frac{1}{2}$ cup icing sugar mixed with
    3 teaspoons ground nutmeg

Cream the butter, sugar and vanilla until light and fluffy. Add the sifted flour and ground almonds and combine well.

Roll dough into balls 3 cm in diameter. Place on lightly greased baking trays and chill for at least 30 minutes.

Preheat oven to 150°C.

Bake for 15–20 minutes. Remove from oven and, while still warm, roll each ball in the icing sugar mixed with nutmeg.

MAKES 60

Oatcake crackers

1 cup plain flour

1 teaspoon bicarbonate of soda

1 teaspoon cream of tartar

1 tablespoon white sugar

125 g cold butter, cut into small pieces

1 cup rolled oats

Preheat oven to 180°C. Lightly grease baking trays.

Sift together the flour, bicarbonate of soda and cream of tartar. Mix in sugar, then rub in the butter with your fingertips until the mixture is crumbly. Stir in the rolled oats and enough hot water to make a stiff dough.

Roll the dough out thinly, cut into squares and place on baking trays. Bake for 10–12 minutes or until lightly golden.

MAKES 30

Old English matrimonials

1½ cups plain flour

pinch of salt

1 teaspoon baking powder

120 g cold butter, cut into small pieces

1¾ cups rolled oats

1 cup soft brown sugar

1½ cups blackberry, raspberry or strawberry jam

Preheat oven to 180°C. Lightly grease a deep 19-cm × 29-cm slice tin.

Sift flour, salt and baking powder into a bowl, add the butter and rub in with your fingertips until crumbly. Stir in the oats and sugar.

Press half the mixture into the tin. Spread jam over the base.

Top with remaining mixture so that it completely covers the jam. Press down lightly.

Bake for 30 minutes or until browned and beginning to bubble around the edges. Cool in the tin before cutting into squares.

MAKES 24

One-pot brownies

120 g butter

60 g dark cooking chocolate

½ teaspoon vanilla extract

1 cup castor sugar

2 eggs

¾ cup plain flour

¾ cup chopped walnuts

Preheat oven to 180°C. Grease and line a 19-cm square cake tin.

Melt the butter and chocolate in a large saucepan over low heat. Remove from heat and cool for a few minutes so the eggs don't scramble when added. Add vanilla and sugar and mix well. Add eggs one at a time, beating well after each addition. Fold in the sifted flour and walnuts.

Pour into prepared tin and bake for about 20 minutes. Cut into squares when cool.

MAKES 18

Open sesame slice

2 cups self-raising wholemeal flour

2 cups desiccated coconut

2 cups white sugar

2 cups rolled oats

2 eggs

240 g butter, melted

2 tablespoons honey

1/3 cup sesame seeds

Preheat oven to 180° C. Lightly grease a 19-cm × 29-cm slice tin.

Combine sifted flour with coconut, sugar and oats. Mix in eggs, then add butter and honey and combine well.

Press into the tin.

Sprinkle sesame seeds evenly over the top of the slice and press in firmly. Bake for 25 minutes or until golden brown.

Cut into squares while warm, but cool in the tray before turning out.

MAKES 24

Orange honey creams

125 g softened butter
½ cup white sugar
1 egg, lightly beaten
4 tablespoons honey
2 cups plain flour
1 teaspoon baking powder
½ teaspoon salt

60 g softened butter
2 teaspoons grated orange zest
2 cups icing sugar
1 tablespoon honey
1 teaspoon orange juice

Preheat oven to 180°C. Lightly grease baking trays.

Cream butter and sugar, then beat in egg and honey. Fold in the sifted dry ingredients.

Spoon mixture into a piping bag with a round tip attached, and pipe onto baking trays in 2-cm wide circles, leaving space between for spreading.

Bake for 15 minutes.

For the filling, cream butter, add the zest, then gradually beat in sifted icing sugar. Add honey and juice and continue beating until smooth.

When biscuits are completely cold, sandwich together with filling.

MAKES 24

Orange thins

250 g softened butter

1¼ cups white sugar

1 egg

grated zest of 1 orange

4 cups plain flour

pinch of salt

1 teaspoon ground cinnamon

½ teaspoon crushed cardamom
seeds

½ cup almond meal

¼ cup orange juice

Preheat oven to 220°C. Lightly grease baking trays.

Cream butter, sugar, egg and zest until light and fluffy. Sift together flour, salt and spices and add to creamed mixture with almond meal and juice. Mix well.

Roll dough out to a thickness of 3 mm and cut out shapes with a floured biscuit cutter. Gather any leftover dough, roll out again, and use to make more biscuits.

Place on prepared trays and bake for 5–7 minutes, or until crisp.

MAKES 120

Parkin

1¾ cups plain flour

1 cup rolled oats

85 g cold butter, cut into small
pieces

⅓ cup soft brown sugar, firmly
packed

1 tablespoon baking powder

½ teaspoon mixed spice

1 tablespoon boiling water

2 tablespoons golden syrup

blanched almonds, split in half,
or mixed peel, for decorating

Preheat oven to 180°C. Lightly grease baking trays.

Combine sifted flour and oats. Rub in butter with your fingertips until crumbly.
Add sugar, baking powder and mixed spice and mix well.

Add boiling water to the golden syrup and mix this into the dry ingredients.

Roll mixture into balls the size of a walnut. Place on baking tray and press
a blanched almond half or a piece of peel into the centre of each.

Bake for 15 minutes.

MAKES 30

Parmesan croissants

¾ cup softened butter

2 cups cottage cheese

2 cups plain flour

pinch of onion or garlic salt

1 cup finely grated parmesan cheese, plus extra for sprinkling

Cream the butter and cottage cheese until smooth. Add the sifted flour and salt and mix well.

Chill for 1 hour, or until easy to handle.

Preheat oven to 200°C. Lightly grease baking trays.

Divide dough into three or four portions. Roll each out to a circle 23 cm in diameter.

Sprinkle each round with parmesan cheese and cut into 8 wedges.

To make the croissants, start with the rounded side of each wedge and roll towards the point. Place point-side down on baking trays and shape into crescents. Sprinkle tops lightly with extra cheese.

Bake 20–25 minutes or until golden. Immediately remove from baking trays and cool on a wire rack.

MAKES 32

Passionfruit biscuits

60 g softened butter

¾ cup icing sugar

pulp of 4 passionfruit (about
⅓ cup pulp)

1¼ cups self-raising flour

1 cup cornflour

FILLING

60 g softened butter

¾ cup icing sugar

pulp of 1 passionfruit
(about 1 tablespoon pulp)

Cream butter and icing sugar until light and fluffy. Add passionfruit pulp and sifted flours. Mix well, then chill mixture until firm.

Preheat oven to 180°C. Lightly grease baking trays.

Roll biscuit dough into small balls. Place on baking trays and flatten with a fork.

Bake for 12–15 minutes.

For the filling, cream butter and icing sugar, then add just enough passionfruit pulp to produce a spreading consistency. Once biscuits are cold, sandwich together with filling.

MAKES 70

Passionfruit cream–cheese slice

1 cup plain flour

2 tablespoons icing sugar

125 g cold butter, cut into small
    pieces

3 teaspoons gelatine

¼ cup water

500 g cream cheese, chopped

280 g lemon butter

⅓ cup custard powder

1 cup castor sugar

2 tablespoons milk

1½ cups water

1 tablespoon butter, extra

2 tablespoons lemon juice

pulp of 4 passionfruit
    (about ⅓ cup pulp)

Preheat oven to 180°C. Lightly grease a 20-cm × 30-cm lamington tin.

For the base, blend the sifted flour and icing sugar with the butter in
a food processor until combined.

Press dough into tin and bake for 20 minutes. Cool.

For the filling, sprinkle the gelatine over the water in a cup. Stand cup in
a small saucepan of simmering water and stir until the gelatine dissolves.
Beat cream cheese until smooth, then add the gelatine and lemon butter.
Beat again until well combined. Spread over the cooked base.

For the topping, combine custard powder, sugar, milk and water in a small saucepan and heat until mixture boils and thickens. Take off the heat and stir in the butter, then let cool for 10 minutes. Stir in the lemon juice and passionfruit pulp, and pour over the slice.

Chill in the refrigerator until set, then cut into large squares.

MAKES 12

Passionfruit fingers

BASE

¾ cup softened butter

1 cup icing sugar

pulp of 4 passionfruit
  (about ⅓ cup pulp)

1½ cups self-raising flour

1 cup cornflour

pinch of salt

ICING

90 g butter, melted

2 cups icing sugar

pulp of 2 passionfruit
  (about 2 tablespoons pulp)

Preheat oven to 180°C. Lightly grease a 19-cm × 29-cm slice tin.

For the base, cream the butter and sifted icing sugar until light and fluffy, then beat in the passionfruit pulp. Add the sifted flour, cornflour and salt and mix well to combine.

Press into prepared tin and bake for 30 minutes.

To make passionfruit icing, beat together the butter, sifted icing sugar and passionfruit pulp until smooth. Once slice is cool, top with icing and cut into fingers.

MAKES 24

Peanut crunch biscuits

75 g softened butter

1 cup soft brown sugar, firmly packed

4 tablespoons crunchy peanut butter

1 egg

⅓ cup rice flour

3 tablespoons cornflour

½ teaspoon bicarbonate of soda

¼ teaspoon cream of tartar

½ teaspoon ground cinnamon

½ cup chopped peanuts

¼ cup ground almonds

¼ cup fine polenta

Preheat oven to 180°C. Lightly grease baking trays.

Cream butter, sugar and peanut butter until smooth, then beat in the egg.

In a separate bowl, sift together flours, bicarbonate of soda, cream of tartar and cinnamon. Stir in peanuts, almonds and polenta, then fold into the creamed mixture.

Divide dough into walnut-sized pieces and place on trays. Flatten with a fork.

Bake for 12–15 minutes, or until the edges are light brown.

MAKES 30 | GLUTEN FREE

Peanut slice

125 g butter

4 tablespoons golden syrup

4 tablespoons crunchy peanut butter

180 g wholemeal biscuits, crushed

Lightly grease a 19-cm square tin.

Stir the butter and golden syrup in a saucepan over medium heat until the butter melts.

Remove from the heat and immediately add the peanut butter, beating well to combine.

Add crushed biscuits and mix until a soft dough forms.

Press into tin and smooth the top. Chill for at least 2 hours before cutting into squares and turning out of the tin.

MAKES 16 | NO BAKE

Polenta fruit biscuits

250 g softened butter

1 cup icing sugar

½ cup polenta

1 egg, separated

2 cups plain flour

mixed crystallised fruit (ginger, cherries,
   pawpaw, pineapple, etc.), for decorating

Preheat oven to 180° C. Lightly grease baking trays.

Cream the butter and sugar until light and fluffy. Add polenta and mix well to combine, then stir in the egg yolk.

Beat egg white until stiff peaks form, then fold into the mixture. Fold in the sifted flour.

Roll teaspoonfulls of mixture into balls and place onto prepared trays. Press a piece of crystallised fruit into the centre of each biscuit. Bake for 10 minutes or until golden.

MAKES 48

Pooh's peanut crisps

2 tablespoons honey

¾ cup crunchy peanut butter

1 cup water

3 cups wholemeal flour

pinch of salt

Preheat oven to 200°C. Lightly grease baking trays.

Mix together honey, peanut butter and water. Add sifted flour and salt and mix to form a stiff dough.

On a very lightly floured surface, roll dough out very thinly. Cut into 6-cm × 3-cm rectangles and prick all over with a fork.

Bake for 10–12 minutes or until crisp.

MAKES 30

Portuguese pine nut biscuits

1 cup cornflour

¾ cup plain flour

½ teaspoon ground cinnamon

200 g pine nuts

90 g butter, melted

⅔ cup castor sugar

4 eggs

pinch of salt

Preheat oven to 190°C. Lightly grease baking trays and dust with flour.

Combine sifted flours and cinnamon with all other ingredients in a bowl – reserving a handful of the pine nuts – and mix until well combined.

Roll dough into small balls, press a few of the reserved pine nuts onto the top of each biscuit and place on prepared trays.

Bake in the oven for 12–15 minutes, or until golden brown.

MAKES 36

Posh choc-shortbread squares

BASE

1 cup self-raising flour

¼ cup white sugar

½ cup desiccated coconut

115 g butter, melted

TOPPING

1 cup icing sugar

1 tablespoon cocoa

1 cup desiccated coconut

60 g butter, melted

3 tablespoons condensed milk

Preheat oven to 180°C. Lightly grease a 19-cm × 29-cm slice tin.

For the base, combine sifted flour, sugar and coconut, then pour over melted butter and mix well.

Press into the tin and bake for 15 minutes.

For the topping, sift together icing sugar and cocoa, then add remaining ingredients and combine well. Spread over the base while still hot.

Cool, then cut into squares.

MAKES 24

Pumpkin date puffs

185 g softened butter

1 cup white sugar

2 eggs

½ teaspoon vanilla extract

1 cup cold mashed pumpkin

1 cup self-raising flour

1½ cups plain flour

pinch of salt

½ teaspoon bicarbonate of soda

¼ teaspoon ground nutmeg

¼ teaspoon mixed spice

1 cup dates, chopped

½ cup walnuts, chopped

Preheat oven to 190°C. Lightly grease baking trays.

Cream butter and sugar until light and fluffy. Gradually beat in the eggs and vanilla, then the mashed pumpkin.

Sift together the flours, salt, bicarbonate of soda and spices. Add to the pumpkin mixture and mix well. Stir in the dates and walnuts.

Drop dessertspoonfuls of mixture onto baking trays and bake for 10–12 minutes.

MAKES 40

Raspberry drops

125 g softened butter

¾ cup white sugar

¼ teaspoon vanilla extract

2 eggs, beaten

1¼ cups plain flour

¼ cup cornflour

½ cup desiccated coconut

raspberry jam, for filling

Preheat oven to 180°C. Lightly grease baking trays.

Cream butter and sugar until light and fluffy. Stir in vanilla extract and eggs. Add sifted flours and coconut. Beat until well combined.

Roll mixture into small balls and place on baking trays. Press a hole into the centre of each biscuit using the end of a teaspoon and fill with raspberry jam.

Bake for 15 minutes. Cool on trays.

MAKES 30

Refrigerator biscuits

185 g softened butter

1 cup soft brown sugar,
   firmly packed

1 egg

1 teaspoon vanilla extract

2¼ cups plain flour

½ teaspoon salt

½ teaspoon baking powder

egg white, for brushing

castor sugar, for sprinkling

Cream the butter and sugar until light and fluffy. Add egg and vanilla and beat well.

In a separate bowl sift together flour, salt and baking powder, then stir into creamed mixture.

Roll mixture into long logs about 5 cm in diameter. Wrap tightly in foil and chill in the refrigerator until cold.

Preheat oven to 180°C. Lightly grease baking trays.

Cut dough into thin slices. Place on baking tray, brush each slice with egg white and sprinkle with castor sugar.

Bake for 7–10 minutes.

(This biscuit dough can be stored in the refrigerator for up to 2 weeks, or frozen for 2 months.)

Before refrigerating, divide dough into five portions. Leave the first portion plain. To the second portion add 2 teaspoons instant coffee granules dissolved in a little water. To the third portion add ⅓ cup desiccated coconut and ½ teaspoon lemon essence. To the fourth portion add 1 teaspoon ground ginger, then top each biscuit round with a piece of crystallised ginger. To the final portion add ½ tablespoon cocoa and ½ teaspoon cinnamon, then top each biscuit round with a chocolate button or almond.

MAKES 60

Rich chocolate shortbread crescents

250 g softened butter

4 tablespoons icing sugar

1 cup cornflour

¾ cup plain flour

2 tablespoons cocoa

90 g dark cooking chocolate, chopped

Preheat oven to 180°C. Lightly grease baking trays.

Cream butter and sifted icing sugar until light and fluffy. Add sifted cornflour, flour and cocoa and combine well.

Put mixture into a piping bag fitted with 1-cm star tip. Pipe onto trays in small crescents (about 3 cm long) and bake for 12 minutes.

Cool on trays and do not decorate until completely cold.

To decorate, melt chocolate in a double boiler over simmering water, or on MEDIUM in the microwave. Drizzle over the top of the crescents, or dip the ends of each cresent into the chocolate. Allow to set before storing in an airtight container.

MAKES 30

Rocky road

375 g milk chocolate, chopped

30 g white vegetable shortening, chopped

200 g pink and white marshmallows, chopped

⅓ cup desiccated coconut

⅓ cup glacé cherries, chopped

⅓ cup macadamia nuts, chopped

Grease and line a 20-cm square cake tin.

Melt chocolate and shortening in a double boiler over simmering water, or on MEDIUM in the microwave.

Combine melted chocolate with remaining ingredients and mix well. Pour into tin.

Freeze for 20 minutes or until set, and cut into pieces to serve.

MAKES 36

Rose royal slice

BASE

1 cup plain flour

1 cup self-raising flour

125 g cold butter, cut into small
  pieces

½ cup white sugar

1 egg, beaten

½ teaspoon vanilla extract

FILLING

1 cup water

2 dessertspoons gelatine

1 cup white sugar

pinch of cream of tartar

few drops red food colouring

TOPPING

250 g white vegetable shortening

1 cup drinking chocolate powder

Preheat oven to 180°C. Lightly grease a 19-cm × 29-cm slice tin.

For the base, sift flours together, then rub in butter with your fingertips until crumbly. Add sugar, egg and vanilla and mix to a firm dough.

Press into tin and bake for about 20 minutes, or until golden. Allow to cool.

For the marshmallow filling, pour water into a saucepan and sprinkle over gelatine. Leave to soak for a few minutes. Add sugar and bring to boil. Reduce heat and simmer for 10 minutes. >

Add cream of tartar and mix. Remove from heat. When liquid is cool, add a few drops of food colouring and beat with an electric mixer until thick and pink. Pour over base and leave to set.

For the topping, melt vegetable shortening in a double boiler over simmering water or on MEDIUM in the microwave, then mix in drinking chocolate.

Pour topping over marshmallow layer. Leave to cool. Cut into squares once completely set.

MAKES 36

Sara's apricot slice

2 cups self-raising flour

¾ cup castor sugar

125 g cold butter, cut into small
    pieces

1 egg, beaten

apricot jam, for spreading

1 egg, beaten

⅓ cup castor sugar

2 cups desiccated coconut

Preheat oven to 180°C. Lightly grease a 19-cm × 29-cm slice tin.

For the base, mix sifted flour and sugar. Rub in the butter with your fingertips until crumbly. Add the beaten egg and mix to a stiff dough.

Press into tin and spread with a layer of jam.

For the topping, mix all ingredients together. Sprinkle over slice.

Bake for about 30 minutes. Cool in tin and then cut into squares.

MAKES 36

Savoury biscotti

3½ cups plain flour

1 teaspoon baking powder

1 teaspoon salt

½ teaspoon freshly ground
black pepper

½ cup grated parmesan cheese

1 tablespoons dried rosemary

1 teaspoon dried oregano or
marjoram

3 eggs

⅔ cup water

Preheat oven to 180°C. Lightly grease baking trays.

In a large bowl, combine the sifted flour, baking powder, salt and pepper with the cheese and herbs.

In a separate bowl, beat the eggs with the water. Add to the dry mixture and mix until combined.

On a lightly floured surface, knead dough until smooth. Divide dough into three portions. Roll each portion into a log about 3 cm in diameter.

Place logs on baking tray and flatten slightly. Bake for 30 minutes.

Turn off oven, remove logs and set aside to cool for 10 minutes. Slice logs diagonally into 1-cm thick slices, then return to the oven for another 20–30 minutes, or until crisp.

MAKES 24

Schoolboy squares

1 cup self-raising flour

1 dessertspoon cocoa

3 Weet-Bix biscuits, crushed

½ cup white sugar

1 cup desiccated coconut

½ cup currants

125 g butter, melted

chocolate glacé icing (page 241)

Preheat oven to 180°C. Lightly grease a 19-cm × 29-cm slice tin.

Sift together flour and cocoa, then mix in other dry ingredients. Pour over melted butter and combine well.

Press mixture into tin.

Bake for 10–15 minutes or until golden. While still warm, ice with chocolate icing and cut into bars.

MAKES 30

Scottish oatcakes

100 g rolled oats

½ teaspoon salt

pinch of bicarbonate of soda

1 tablespoon vegetable oil

2 tablespoons hot water

Preheat oven to 180°C. Lightly grease baking trays.

Place oats, salt and bicarbonate of soda in a large bowl. Stir in the oil and hot water and mix to a firm dough.

Roll out on a lightly floured surface and use a 7.5-cm cutter to cut out rounds. Gather any leftover dough, roll out again and use to make more rounds. You should end up with 8 rounds. Cut each of these into quarters.

Place on trays and bake for 8–10 minutes or until golden and crisp.

MAKES 32

Scrummy six-layer slice

125 g butter, melted

1 cup sweet biscuit crumbs

1 cup desiccated coconut

375 g chocolate chips

1 × 395-g tin condensed milk

1 cup nuts (almonds, hazelnuts, etc.),
  roughly chopped

Preheat oven to 180°C. Lightly grease and line a 19-cm × 29-cm slice tin.

Each of the ingredients in this slice forms a layer. First pour the melted butter into the tin, then sprinkle over the biscuit crumbs, followed by the coconut. Next scatter over the chocolate chips in an even layer, then pour over the condensed milk. The final layer is made of the nuts.

Bake for about 30 minutes. Cool, then cut into fingers.

MAKES 36

Sesame potato biscuits

2 cups plain flour

1½ teaspoons salt

240 g cold butter, cut into small
  pieces

1 cup cold mashed potato

3 egg yolks

2 tablespoons sour cream

1 egg, extra

¼ cup sesame seeds

Sift together flour and salt. Using your fingertips, rub in the butter until crumbly.

Stir in mashed potato, egg yolks and sour cream.

Knead dough for 1 minute until smooth, then wrap in foil and chill for 20 minutes. Repeat this kneading and chilling process three times.

Preheat oven to 200°C. Lightly grease baking trays.

Roll out dough to 5 mm in thickness and cut into rounds using a biscuit cutter. Beat extra egg and brush it over biscuits. Sprinkle with sesame seeds.

Bake for 15–20 minutes until lightly brown.

MAKES 24

Sesame snack bars

1½ cups white sugar

¾ cup water

75 g sesame seeds, toasted

1 teaspoon ground cinnamon

pinch of ground cloves

½ teaspoon lemon juice

Gently heat sugar and water in a saucepan until sugar has dissolved, then bring to the boil. Continue boiling, without stirring, until the syrup begins to turn golden brown.

Add the remaining ingredients and continue boiling for 3 minutes, stirring continuously.

Remove from the heat, pour onto a wet marble slab (or chopping board) and using a wet rolling pin, roll out to a thickness of about 1 cm. Using a palette knife, quickly lever off the slab and cut into bars. (Don't worry if it sets too quickly – you can simply leave it to harden completely, then snap into chunks.)

MAKES 24 | GLUTEN FREE | NO BAKE

Shona's midnight munchies

100 g butter

¼ cup castor sugar

¼ cup dark treacle

1 cup plain flour

2 teaspoons baking powder

½ teaspoon salt

100 g rolled oats

¾ cup sultanas

Preheat oven to 180°C. Lightly grease and line a 19-cm × 29-cm slice tin.

Place the butter, sugar and treacle into a saucepan and heat gently until butter has melted and sugar dissolved.

In a bowl, sift together flour, baking powder and salt. Mix in oats and sultanas, then pour over butter mixture. Mix thoroughly.

Press mixture into prepared tin and bake for 20 minutes.

MAKES 24

Shortbread

1¼ cups gluten-free flour mix (page xiii)

¼ cup white sugar

100 g cold butter, cut into small pieces

Preheat oven to 150°C. Lightly grease a 20-cm fluted flan tin.

Combine sifted flour and sugar. Using your fingertips, rub in the butter until a fine crumbly mixture forms. Roll dough into a ball.

Press into tray. Score diamond shapes. Bake for 30–40 minutes until light brown. Cool in the tray, then cut along the scored lines.

VARIATIONS

For ginger shortbread, add 1 dessertspoon ground ginger with the flour. For cinnamon shortbread, add 1 dessertspoon ground cinnamon with the flour.

MAKES 8 | GLUTEN FREE

Smoked paprika puffs

4 tablespoons self-raising flour
pinch of salt
pinch of smoked paprika, plus extra for sprinkling
80 g butter, melted
4 tablespoons grated tasty or parmesan cheese
sesame seeds or desiccated coconut, for coating

Preheat oven to 180° C. Lightly grease baking trays.

Sift together flour, salt and paprika. Add butter and cheese and mix until well combined.

Roll dough into small balls, then roll in sesame seeds or coconut to coat.

Place balls on baking trays and bake for 15 minutes, or until golden brown.

MAKES 36

Snickerdoodles

60 g softened butter

¾ cup castor sugar

1 egg

¾ cup plain flour

½ cup self-raising flour

pinch of salt

¼ cup wheatgerm

½ teaspoon vanilla extract

2 tablespoons castor sugar mixed with 2 teaspoons ground cinnamon, for coating

Preheat oven to 190°C. Lightly grease baking trays.

Cream butter and sugar until light and fluffy. Add egg and mix well. Stir in sifted flours, salt, wheatgerm and vanilla until well combined.

Roll mixture into 2-cm balls, then roll the balls in the cinnamon sugar to coat.

Place balls on trays, leaving space between each for spreading. Bake for 10–12 minutes.

MAKES 24

Snow on the trees

25 g butter

½ cup castor sugar

2 tablespoons cocoa

1 egg, beaten

2 tablespoons desiccated coconut,
plus extra for sprinkling

2 cups sweet biscuit crumbs

¼ cup dates, chopped

¼ cup glacé cherries, chopped

glacé icing (page 241)

few drops green food colouring

Preheat oven to 180°C. Grease a 23-cm square cake tin.

Place butter, sugar and cocoa in a small saucepan and heat for 2 minutes. Remove from heat and cool for a few minutes so egg doesn't scramble when added. Mix in egg, coconut, biscuits, dates and cherries.

Press mixture firmly into tin and bake for 15 minutes.

Make icing and stir in a few drops of green food colouring. When slice is cold, top with a thin layer of icing, then sprinkle with extra coconut. Cut into squares to serve.

MAKES 24

Sour cream apple slice

BASE

125 g butter, melted

1 × 600-g packet vanilla cake mix

1 cup desiccated coconut

FILLING

500 g stewed apple (or pie apple), well drained

TOPPING

1 egg, beaten

1 × 300-ml carton sour cream

ground cinnamon, for sprinkling

castor sugar, for sprinkling

Preheat oven to 180°C. Lightly grease a 25-cm × 30-cm Swiss roll tin.

For the base, mix melted butter with cake mix and coconut until well combined.

Press into tin and bake in oven for 10–15 minutes until golden brown. Set aside to cool. (Leave oven on.)

Spread apple filling evenly over base.

For the topping, fold egg into sour cream. Pour sour cream mixture evenly over apple and sprinkle with cinnamon and castor sugar.

Bake for a further 20 minutes. Cool in tin then cut into slices.

MAKES 36

Spiced jumbles

1 cup softened butter

1 cup white sugar

1 teaspoon ground nutmeg

1 teaspoon ground cinnamon

1 teaspoon ground ginger

1 egg, beaten

3 cups plain flour

Preheat oven to 180°C.

Cream butter and sugar until very light. Add spices, then beat in egg.

Add sifted flour a cup at a time to form a soft dough that is not sticky, adding more flour if necessary.

Roll out on a lightly floured surface to 5 mm in thickness, and then cut into shapes with biscuit cutters. (Alternatively, you can roll small pieces into long ropes about 2 cm in diameter and then twist them into figure of eights.)

Bake on ungreased baking trays for 12–15 minutes.

MAKES 36

Spicy apple slice

125 g butter

½ cup castor sugar, plus extra for sprinkling

1 egg

1 cup plain flour

1 teaspoon cinnamon

1 teaspoon ground ginger

1½ cups stewed apple (or pie apple),
    well drained

Preheat oven to 180° C. Lightly grease a 19-cm × 29-cm slice tin.
Cream butter and sugar until light and fluffy. Add egg and beat well.

In a separate bowl sift together flour, cinnamon and ginger. Fold into
creamed mixture.

Spread half the mixture into the tin. Cover with the apple and then spread
remaining mixture on top. Brush with water and sprinkle generously with
castor sugar.

Bake for about 45 minutes, or until golden brown. Serve warm or cold.

MAKES 16

Spicy slice

250 g softened butter

1 cup soft brown sugar

1 teaspoon vanilla extract

1 egg, separated

2 cups plain flour

1 teaspoon ground cinnamon

¼ teaspoon ground ginger

¼ teaspoon ground nutmeg

1 cup ground walnuts

Preheat oven to 180°C. Lightly grease a 19-cm × 29-cm slice tin and dust with flour.

Cream butter, sugar and vanilla until light and fluffy. Add egg yolk and beat well.

Sift together the flour and spices, and stir into the creamed mixture. Mix in half the ground walnuts.

Spread mixture into the prepared tin.

Beat egg white until frothy, but not stiff, and spread over the mixture. Sprinkle with the remaining nuts.

Bake for 25 minutes. Cool slightly, then cut into squares.

MAKES 24

Squashed fly slice

2 sheets frozen shortcrust pastry

½ cup currants

½ cup raisins, chopped

1½ cups sultanas, chopped

1 tablespoon sherry

1 egg, lightly beaten

white sugar, for sprinkling

Preheat oven to 180°C. Grease and line a baking tray.

Lay a sheet of pastry on the tray and spread the combined fruit evenly across it. Sprinkle with the sherry.

Place remaining sheet of pastry over the top, and press down to remove any trapped air. Press edges of pastry together with a fork to seal.

Prick pastry all over with a fork, then brush with egg and sprinkle with sugar.

Bake for about 10 minutes, then reduce the temperature to 160°C and cook for a further 20 minutes, or until golden brown.

When cool, cut into squares.

MAKES 16

Sugared Brazil bars

BASE

60 g cold butter, cut into small
  pieces

1 cup plain flour

FILLING

¼ cup soft brown sugar

2 eggs, beaten

1 cup Brazil nuts, finely chopped

½ cup desiccated coconut

1 teaspoon vanilla extract

TOPPING

185 g cooking chocolate,
  chopped

⅓ cup golden syrup

1 tablespoon water

½ cup Brazil nuts, finely chopped

Preheat oven to 180°C. Lightly grease a 23-cm square cake tin.

For the base, rub butter into sifted flour with your fingertips until crumbly. Press into tin and bake for 15 minutes. Remove. (Leave oven on.)

For the filling, beat sugar and eggs until frothy, then mix in nuts, coconut and vanilla. Spread filling over base and bake for a further 15 minutes. Set aside to cool in the tin.

For the topping, melt chocolate in a double boiler over simmering water, or on MEDIUM in the microwave. Add golden syrup and water and blend well. Spread topping over the slice and sprinkle with remaining nuts. Let stand until firm, then cut into bars.

MAKES 24

Sultana choc-chip biscuits

125 g softened butter
1½ cups soft brown sugar
½ teaspoon vanilla extract
1 egg, beaten
1¾ cups self-raising flour
½ cup sultanas
½ cup chocolate chips

Preheat oven to 180'C. Lightly grease baking trays.

Cream butter, sugar and vanilla until light and fluffy. Beat in egg, then stir in sifted flour, sultanas and chocolate chips to form a stiff dough.

Roll dough into small balls and place on baking trays. Flatten slightly with a fork.

Bake for 15–20 minutes, until lightly browned.

MAKES 36

Sultana slice

125 g butter
1 cup soft brown sugar
1 egg, beaten
2 cups sultanas
1½ cups self-raising flour

Preheat oven to 190°C. Lightly grease a 20-cm × 30-cm lamington tin.

Melt the butter in a saucepan, then add sugar and stir until dissolved. Remove from heat and cool for a few minutes so egg doesn't scramble when added. Mix in egg, sultanas and sifted flour. Mix thoroughly.

Press into prepared tin and bake for 20 minutes, or until a golden crust has formed.

Cool before cutting into squares or bars.

MAKES 24

Sun-dried tomato cheese squares

BASE

75 g butter, melted

150 g wholemeal breadcrumbs

FILLING

125 g baby spinach leaves

100 g feta, crumbled

100 g mozzarella, diced

12 sun-dried tomatoes, chopped

3 eggs, beaten

1 × 375-g tin evaporated milk

2 tablespoons chopped fresh
   basil leaves

salt and freshly ground black
   pepper

Preheat oven to 200°C. Lightly grease a deep 19-cm × 29-cm slice tin.

For the base, mix melted butter and breadcrumbs and press into the base of the tin. Bake for 15 minutes. Set aside to cool.

For the filling, cover the cooled base with a layer of spinach leaves, then sprinkle over half the cheese and sun-dried tomatoes. Cover with remaining spinach, then remaining cheese and tomato.

Beat the eggs with the evaporated milk and basil and season well with salt and pepper. Pour over slice.

Bake for 20 minutes, then reduce heat to 180°C and cook for a further 30 minutes or until set and golden.

MAKES 36

Sweet sesame biscuits

¾ cup self-raising flour

1¼ cups plain flour

¼ teaspoon salt

185 g cold butter, cut into
  small pieces

¾ cup castor sugar

1 egg yolk

1 teaspoon vanilla extract

1 tablespoon milk

125 g sesame seeds, toasted

Preheat oven to 180°C. Lightly grease baking trays.

Sift together flours and salt, then rub in butter with your fingertips until crumbly.

Add sugar, egg yolk, vanilla and milk and mix to form a soft dough.

Roll teaspoonfuls of mixture into balls about 2 cm in diameter. Roll balls in sesame seeds, place on baking trays and press down gently with the back of a spoon.

Bake for 12–15 minutes or until golden.

MAKES 48

Swiss lemon slice

1 cup self-raising flour
1 cup desiccated coconut
115 g butter, melted
⅓ cup soft brown sugar
lemon glacé icing (page 241)

Preheat oven to 180°C. Lightly grease a 19-cm × 29-cm slice tin.

Sift self-raising flour, then mix with coconut, butter and sugar.

Press into the tin. Bake for 15 minutes. When cold, ice with lemon icing.

MAKES 24

Sydney specials

125 g butter, melted
1 cup soft brown sugar
1 cup desiccated coconut
2 cups rolled oats

Preheat oven to 180°C. Lightly grease a 23-cm square slab tin.

Mix all ingredients together until well combined. Press into the tin.

Bake for 20 minutes or until golden brown. Cut into slices or squares while still warm.

MAKES 24

Tell my fortune cookies

3 egg whites

½ cup icing sugar

45 g unsalted butter, melted

½ cup plain flour

¼ teaspoon almond essence

strips of non-toxic paper with
    fortunes written on them

Preheat oven to 180°C. Cut a sheet of baking paper to fit your baking tray, then draw three 8-cm circles onto the paper. Place the sheet on the tray.

Beat egg whites until frothy. Add the sifted icing sugar and butter and stir until smooth. Stir in the sifted flour and then add the almond essence. Set mixture aside for 15 minutes.

Using a spatula, spread 1½ teaspoons of the mixture evenly into each circle. Bake for 5 minutes or until starting to colour around the edges.

Remove cookies from the tray one at a time, using a spatula. While still warm, place a fortune in the centre of each cookie. Bring sides up to meet in the middle and press to seal, then bend into a crescent shape.

Pack each cookie into a muffin tray hole or a small glass until set and cold (this will help them keep their shape). Repeat until all mixture is used up.

(You can't bake too many of these cookies at once, as they must be hot in order to be shaped. Prepare the next tray while the previous one is cooking.)

MAKES 20

Three-layer apricot rough

BASE

¾ cup self-raising flour

¾ cup desiccated coconut

¾ cup soft brown sugar

90 g butter, melted

FILLING

125 g dried apricots, chopped

2 cups desiccated coconut

¾ cup condensed milk

TOPPING

125 g dark cooking chocolate

30 g white vegetable shortening

Preheat oven to 180°C. Lightly grease a 23-cm square slab tin.

For the base, mix sifted flour with other ingredients until well combined. Press into the tin. Bake for 15 minutes.

For the filling, place apricots into a small saucepan and cover with water. Simmer for a few minutes, until tender. Drain.

Mix apricots with coconut and condensed milk, then spread over the warm biscuit base.

For the topping, melt the chocolate and shortening in a double boiler over simmering water, or on MEDIUM in the microwave. Stir until smooth, then spread over the apricot filling. Chill before cutting into small squares.

MAKES 36

Toffee crackle fruit slice

BASE

125 g softened butter

½ cup white sugar

1 teaspoon vanilla extract

1 egg yolk

1½ cups plain flour

FILLING

1 × 375-g packet mixed dried
    fruit

60 g glacé cherries

2 tablespoons plain flour

1 egg

2 tablespoons soft brown sugar

1 teaspoon vanilla extract

1 tablespoon brandy

TOPPING

1 cup white sugar

½ cup water

1 tablespoon butter

Preheat oven to 180°C. Lightly grease a 19-cm × 29-cm slice tin.

For the base, cream butter, sugar and vanilla until light and fluffy. Add egg yolk and beat well. Add sifted flour and beat until well combined.

Spread mixture into tin and bake for about 15 minutes, or until golden. Set aside to cool a little. (Leave oven on.)

For the filling, combine the dried fruit, cherries and sifted flour. In a separate bowl, beat together the egg, sugar, vanilla and brandy. Add egg mixture to fruit mixture and combine thoroughly. >

Spread fruit mixture over base. Return to oven and bake for 20 minutes.

For the toffee topping, combine sugar and water in saucepan. Stir over low heat until sugar has dissolved, then bring to the boil. Continue boiling gently, without stirring, until it turns a light toffee colour. Remove from heat, add butter and swirl pan until butter has melted.

While slice is still hot, pour toffee evenly over the top. Leave to set slightly, then score squares with a sharp knife. Cool in the tin before cutting into squares.

MAKES 36

Treacle flapjacks

75 g butter

100 g castor sugar

1 tablespoon treacle

1 cup gluten-free corn flakes

100 g millet flakes (precooked variety)

100 g rice flakes (precooked variety)

2 tablespoons mixed nuts, chopped (optional)

Preheat oven to 180°C. Lightly grease a 19-cm × 29-cm slice tin.

In a large saucepan, combine the butter, sugar and treacle over low heat until sugar has dissolved.

Stir in the Corn Flakes, millet and rice flakes, and nuts (if using). Spread mixture into the tin.

Bake for 30–45 minutes until golden brown. Cut into fingers while still hot, but do not remove from tin until cold.

MAKES 16 | GLUTEN FREE

Treacle snaps

185 g softened butter

1 cup white sugar, plus extra for
    coating

¼ cup treacle

1 egg

2 cups plain flour

pinch of salt

1 teaspoon bicarbonate of soda

1 teaspoon ground cinnamon

1 teaspoon ground cloves

1 teaspoon ground ginger

Cream butter, sugar and treacle until light and fluffy. Beat in the egg.
In a separate bowl, sift together flour, salt, bicarbonate of soda and spices.
Add to creamed mixture and beat until combined. Chill for 1 hour.

Preheat oven to 190°C. Lightly grease baking trays.

Roll spoonfuls of mixture into balls 2.5 cm in diameter, then roll in sugar
to coat.

Place on trays and bake for about 10 minutes, or until lightly browned.

Cool on trays for 5 minutes, then transfer to a wire rack.

MAKES 40

Tuna lunchbox slice

½ cup olive oil

675 g potatoes, diced

2 bay leaves

1 onion, chopped

2 cloves garlic, chopped

1 cup frozen peas

1 red capsicum, diced

salt and black pepper

2 teaspoons paprika

1 × 425-g tin tuna, drained

½ × 400-g tin whole peeled
tomatoes

1 cup white wine

handful fresh parsley, chopped

500 g frozen shortcrust pastry
sheets

milk, for brushing

Heat oil in a large frying pan and stir-fry potatoes and bay leaves for
5 minutes. Add onion and garlic and cook for 5 minutes. Add peas and
capsicum and cook for 5 minutes. Season with salt, pepper and paprika.

Add tuna, tomatoes, wine and parsley, and simmer until most of the liquid
has evaporated. Remove bay leaves and set aside to cool.

Preheat oven to 200°C. Lightly grease a large shallow baking tin.

Cut pastry sheets to cover base and sides of tin. Pour in tuna mix. Moisten
pastry edges and cover filling with more pastry, pressing the top and bottom
edges together with a fork to seal. Brush the top with milk and bake until
golden brown. Cut into squares and eat hot or cold.

MAKES 16

Vanilla drops

185 g softened butter

1¼ cups white sugar

1 teaspoon vanilla extract

2 eggs, beaten

3 cups plain flour

3 teaspoons baking powder

¾ teaspoon salt

⅔ cup milk

Preheat oven to 180°C. Lightly grease baking trays.

Cream butter and sugar until light and fluffy. Add vanilla, then gradually beat in eggs.

In a separate bowl, sift together flour, baking powder and salt. Gradually fold into the creamed mixture, alternating with the milk.

Drop teaspoonfuls of mixture onto prepared trays. Bake for about 15 minutes or until pale golden.

VARIATIONS

For chocolate drops, add 60 g melted chocolate when you add the vanilla. For cherry drops, add ⅓ cup chopped glacé cherries with the flour and milk. For nut drops, add ½ cup chopped nuts (almonds, walnuts or pecans) with the flour and milk. For orange drops, add 2 teaspoons finely grated orange zest with the flour, and replace milk with orange juice.

MAKES 60

Walnut whiteys

225 g white cooking chocolate

75 g butter

200 g condensed milk

3 eggs, separated

1⅓ cups self-raising flour

100 g chocolate-chip biscuits, crushed

100 g walnuts, roughly chopped

225 g white chocolate buttons

Preheat oven to 180°C. Grease and line a 25-cm × 31-cm slice tin.

Melt the white chocolate with the butter in a double boiler over simmering water, or on MEDIUM in the microwave. Set aside to cool.

In a large bowl, combine the condensed milk, egg yolks, sifted flour, biscuit crumbs, nuts and chocolate buttons. Add the melted chocolate and mix well.

Whisk the egg whites until soft peaks form, then gently fold into the mixture.

Pour into prepared tin and bake for 30 minutes or until risen and golden. Cool on a wire rack before cutting into squares.

MAKES 20

White chocolate button biscuits

100 g softened butter

½ cup castor sugar

1 cup soft brown sugar

1 egg

1 teaspoon vanilla extract

1½ cups plain flour

½ teaspoon baking powder

pinch of salt

175 g white chocolate buttons

Preheat oven to 190°C. Line baking trays with baking paper.

Cream butter and sugars until light and fluffy. Whisk together the egg and vanilla and beat into the creamed mixture.

In a separate bowl, sift together the flour, baking powder and salt. Add to the creamed mixture and combine well.

Place chocolate buttons in a plastic bag and break into small pieces using a rolling pin or mallet. Stir chocolate into the mixture.

Roll dough into walnut sized balls. Place onto trays, leaving plenty of space for spreading. Bake for 10–12 minutes.

MAKES 36

White Christmas

1 cup powdered milk

1 cup icing sugar

1 cup Rice Bubbles

1 cup mixed dried fruit

250 g white vegetable shortening, melted

2 teaspoons vanilla extract

Lightly grease a 23-cm square slab tin.

Sift together powdered milk and icing sugar. Mix in Rice Bubbles and dried fruit. Add vegetable shortening and mix well, then stir in vanilla.

Pour into tin. Chill in refrigerator until firm, then cut into small squares.

MAKES 36 | NO BAKE

Wholemeal banana bars

1½ cups self-raising wholemeal
    flour
pinch of salt
1 cup wheatgerm
½ cup soft brown sugar
250 g dates, chopped

1¼ cups milk
125 g butter
2 eggs, beaten
3 bananas, mashed
lemon glacé icing (page 241)

Preheat oven to 190°C. Lightly grease two 19-cm square cake tins.

Combine sifted flour and salt, wheatgerm, sugar and dates in a bowl.

Bring ¼ cup of the milk to the boil in a small saucepan. Add butter
and stir until it melts. Add beaten eggs and remaining milk.

Pour liquid into dry ingredients and beat well. Add mashed banana and
stir until well combined.

Spoon into prepared tins and cook for 40–45 minutes or until risen
and browned.

Once cool, top with lemon icing. Cut into bars.

MAKES 24

Wholemeal crackers

4 cups wholemeal flour

1 teaspoon salt

1½–1¾ cups sour cream

Preheat oven to 180°C. Lightly grease baking trays.

Sift together flour and salt, then add just enough sour cream to make a soft and pliable dough.

On a lightly floured surface, roll out the dough thinly. Cut into squares with a knife, or cut into rounds using a biscuit cutter.

Bake for 10–12 minutes or until pale golden.

MAKES 48

Yoghurt bars

BASE

1 cup wholemeal plain flour

2 tablespoons cold butter, cut
   into small pieces

2 tablespoons water

1 tablespoon freshly squeezed
   lemon juice

FILLING

500 g natural yoghurt

200 g cottage cheese

3 tablespoons honey

¼ cup wholemeal plain flour

1 tablespoon finely grated
   lemon zest

1 tablespoon lemon juice

2 eggs, lightly beaten

TOPPING

60 g butter

1 cup wholemeal self-raising
   flour

¼ cup soft brown sugar

2 tablespoons chopped or flaked
   almonds

Preheat oven to 220°C. Lightly grease a 23-cm square cake tin.

For the base, sift flour into a large mixing bowl. Add butter and rub in with your fingertips until crumbly. Add the water and lemon juice and mix to form a stiff dough.

Knead dough lightly on a floured surface. Roll out and use to line the base of the cake tin. Chill in the refrigerator while preparing the filling.

For the filling, mix together the yogurt, cottage cheese and honey until smooth. Fold in the sifted flour and lemon zest. Add lemon juice and eggs and mix well. Spread over the chilled base.

For the topping, rub butter into sifted flour and sugar until crumbly. Spread over the filling and sprinkle with the nuts.

Place in the preheated oven, then reduce temperature immediately to 200°C and bake for 45 minutes. Cool a little, then refrigerate until cold. Cut into slices to serve.

MAKES 24

Yoyos

190 g softened butter

1/3 cup icing sugar

1 cup plain flour

1 cup custard powder

pinch of salt

1/2 teaspoon vanilla extract

butter icing (page 243) or jam, for spreading

Preheat oven to 180°C. Lightly grease a baking tray.

Cream butter and sifted icing sugar until light and fluffy. In a separate bowl sift together flour, custard powder and salt. Add to creamed mixture with vanilla to form a soft dough.

Roll dough into balls, place onto baking tray and flatten slightly with a fork.

Bake for 15–20 minutes, until a pale beige colour.

Once cold, sandwich biscuits together with jam or butter icing flavoured with a little vanilla extract or lemon essence.

MAKES 36

Zucchini slice

3 large zucchini, finely grated

1 medium onion, finely chopped

1 cup grated tasty cheese

¾ cup self-raising flour

salt and freshly ground black pepper

½ cup vegetable oil

4 eggs, beaten

Preheat oven to 180°C. Grease and line a 19-cm × 29-cm slice tin.

Squeeze the grated zucchini to remove any excess liquid.

In a large bowl, combine the zucchini with the onion, cheese, sifted flour, salt and pepper. Mix the oil with the beaten eggs, then add to the other ingredients and stir to combine.

Pour into tin and bake for 45–50 minutes or until firm to touch and golden brown.

Cut into slices when cold.

MAKES 24

Icing

These icings can be used to decorate any biscuits or slices that require extra topping. Each recipe makes ¾ cup icing.

Glacé icing

Glacé icing is a smooth, glossy icing that should have a fairly runny consistency. It works best when poured over warm slices or biscuits, as the surface becomes dull if you spread it.

2 cups icing sugar

2 tablespoons warm water

food colourings and flavourings (optional)

Sift the icing sugar into a bowl. Gradually add the water, beating until the icing is smooth and thick enough to coat the back of a spoon. Flavour and colour as required and use immediately.

VARIATIONS

For chocolate glacé icing add 60 g melted chocolate, 1 teaspoon melted butter and 1 teaspoon vanilla extract. For coffee glacé icing substitute half of the water with 1 tablespoon strong black coffee or 1 dessertspoon coffee essence. For fruit glacé icing replace the water with 2 tablespoons warmed fruit juice (e.g. lemon, orange or pineapple). >

Butter icing

Butter icing is soft with a matt finish, and it's much richer in flavour than glacé icing. It stays relatively moist and can be used for sandwiching biscuits together.

125 g softened butter

2 cups icing sugar

1–2 tablespoons warm milk

food colourings and flavourings (optional)

Cream the butter in a bowl. Gradually add sifted icing sugar, alternately with the milk, until soft and creamy. Beat in flavouring and colouring, if using.

VARIATIONS

For chocolate butter icing add 60 g melted chocolate (or add 1 tablespoon cocoa with the icing sugar). For fruit butter icing replace the warm milk with 2 tablespoons warmed fruit juice (e.g. lemon, orange or pineapple). >

Vienna icing

Vienna icing is similar to butter icing, but with a dash of alcohol.

2 cups icing sugar

90 g softened butter

2 tablespoons sherry, brandy or other liqueur

Cream the butter in a bowl. Gradually add sifted icing sugar, alternately with the liqueur, until soft and creamy.

Conversions

Celsius	Fahrenheit
150°C	300°F
160°C	320°F
170°C	340°F
180°C	360°F
190°C	375°F
200°C	390°F
220°C	430°F

WEIGHTS

Grams	Ounces
15 g	½ oz
25 g	1 oz
50 g	2 oz
80 g	3 oz
100 g	3.5 oz
150 g	5 oz
175 g	6 oz
250 g	9 oz
375 g	13 oz
500 g	16 oz (1 lb)
750 g	1⅔ lb
1 kg	2 lb

LIQUIDS

Millilitres	Fluid ounces
50 ml	2 fl oz
300 ml	11 fl oz

SIZES

Centimetres	Inches
1 cm	⅖ in
1.5 cm	⅗ in
2 cm	⅘ in
2.5 cm	1 in
3 cm	1⅕ in
4 cm	1⅗ in
5 cm	2 in
6 cm	2⅖
7 cm	2⅘ in
7.5 cm	3 in
8 cm	3 in
9 cm	3½ in
10 cm	4 in
18 cm	7 in
20 cm	8 in
23 cm	9 in
25 cm	10 in

Index

Note: Recipes appear alphabetically in the text.

almond
  Almond Biscotti 3
  Almond Biscuits 5
  Almond Lace Doilies 6
  Almond Shortbread 8
  Amaretti 9
  Apricot Almond Slice 17
  Cherry Macaroons 52
  Cinnamon Macaroons 68
  Lebkuchen 129
  Marzipan Marvels 142
  Tell My Fortune Cookies 218
apple
  Apple and Date Chews 16
  Sour Cream Apple Slice 203
  Spicy Apple Slice 206
apricot *see* dried and candied fruit;
  jam and marmalade

banana
  Animal Biscuits 12
  Banana Nut Biscuits 30
  Wholemeal Banana Bars 233
berries *see* jam and marmalade
brownies
  Butterscotch Brownies 37
  One-pot Brownies 156

caramel
  Caramel Crackle Squares 40
  Caramel-crusted Fruit Slice 41
  Caramel Slice 43
  Golden Slice 104
cereal
  Afghans 2
  Apricot Hazelnut Crunch 22
  Auntie Ruth's Lemon Slice 28

  Bran Biscuits 35
  Caramel Crackle Squares 40
  Chocka Cherry Bars 53
  Cocoa Slice 73
  Coconut Fancies 75
  Double Dip Mars Bar Slice 83
  Florentine Bars 84
  Fruity Cereal Bars 88
  Ginger and Date Slice 93
  Honey Joys 118
  Maraschino Marshmallow Slice 138
  Marshmallow Fingers 140
  Mrs Baillie's Sunflower and Honey
    Squares 148
  Schoolboy Squares 190
  Snickerdoodles 200
  Treacle Flapjacks 223
  White Christmas 231
cheese/cream cheese
  Caraway Crisps 44
  Cheese Straws 48
  Cheese-cream Sandwiches 46
  Ham and Cheese Slice 106
  Herby Cheese Crackers 111
  Parmesan Croissants 163
  Passionfruit Cream-cheese Slice 166
  Savoury Biscotti 189
  Smoked Paprika Puffs 199
  Sun-dried Tomato Cheese Squares 213
  Yoghurt Bars 236
  Zucchini Slice 240
chocolate
  Afghans 2
  American Tollhouse Cookies 11
  Chocolate Butter Icing 243
  Chocolate Chip Cookies 54
  Chocolate Diamonds 56

Chocolate Drops 227
Chocolate Fruit Slice 57
Chocolate Fudge Slice 59
Chocolate Ginger Rounds 60
Chocolate Glacé Icing 241
Chocolate Jam Slice 61
Chocolate Molasses Slice 62
Chocolate Nut Florentines 64
Chocolate Rice Biscuits 65
Chocolate Rocks 67
Cocoa Slice 73
Double Dip Mars Bar Slice 83
Florentine Bars 84
Honeybunch Hearts 116
Jamaica Slice 119
Kiwi Chocolate-iced Slice 126
Marzipan Marvels 142
Mocha Creams 146
Mum's Chocolate Walnut Slice 150
One-pot Brownies 156
Posh Choc-shortbread Squares 176
Rich Chocolate Shortbread Crescents 182
Rocky Road 184
Rose Royal Slice 185
Schoolboy Squares 190
Scrummy Six-layer Slice 192
Sugared Brazil Bars 210
Sultana Choc-chip Biscuits 211
Three-layer Apricot Rough 220
Walnut Whiteys 228
White Chocolate Button Biscuits 230
coconut
    Anzac Biscuits 13
    Anzac Slice 14
    Apricot Meringue Slice 25
    Cherry Coconut Crisps 51
    Chocka Cherry Bars 53
    Chocolate Jam Slice 61
    Cocoa Slice 73
    Coconut Fancies 75
    Coconut Ice Slice 76
    Coconut Rough Slice 78
    Golden Slice 104

Kiwi Chocolate-iced Slice 126
Lucy's Ginger Slice 135
Maraschino Marshmallow Slice 138
Open Sesame Slice 158
Posh Choc-shortbread Squares 176
Sara's Apricot Slice 187
Schoolboy Squares 190
Scrummy Six-layer Slice 192
Snow on the Trees 202
Sour Cream Apple Slice 302
Swiss Lemon Slice 216
Sydney Specials 217
Three-layer Apricot Rough 220
coffee
    Coffee Glacé Icing 24
    Coffee Layer Slice 79
    Coffee Rice Biscuits 65
    Mocha Creams 146

dates
    Apple and Date Chews 16
    Butterscotch Date Biscuits 38
    Ginger and Date Slice 93
    Pumpkin Date Puffs 177
    Snow on the Trees 202
dried and candied fruit
    Apricot, Ginger and Lemon Slice 20
    Apricot Hazelnut Crunch 22
    Apricot Lunchbox Biscuits 23
    Apricot and Sesame Slice 19
    Caramel-crusted Fruit Slice 41
    Cherry Drops 227
    Cherry Macaroons 52
    Chocka Cherry Bars 53
    Chocolate Fruit Slice 57
    Chocolate Fudge Slice 59
    Chocolate Nut Florentines 64
    Cinnamon Mince Slice 70
    Currant Granola Squares 81
    Florentine Bars 84
    Frilled Easter Biscuits 86
    Fruity Cereal Bars 88
    Fudgy Fruit Slice 89

Hodge Podge 113
Jamaica Slice 119
Maraschino Marshmallow Slice 138
Mince Slice 145
Mrs Baillie's Sunflower and Honey
    Squares 148
Polenta Fruit Biscuits 172
Rocky Road 184
Shona's Midnight Munchies 197
Snow on the Trees 202
Squashed Fly Slice 208
Sultana Choc-chip Biscuits 211
Sultana Slice 212
Three-layer Apricot Rough 220
Toffee Crackle Fruit Slice 221
White Christmas 231

ginger
Apricot, Ginger and Lemon Slice 20
Chocolate Ginger Rounds 60
Ginger Biscuits 94
Ginger Crunch 98
Ginger and Date Slice 93
Ginger Nuts 99
Ginger Shortbread 198
Ginger Sticks 101
Gingerbread Men 95
Gingerbread Squares 96
Lucy's Ginger Slice 135

honey
Frilled Easter Biscuits 86
Honey Joys 118
Honeybunch Hearts 116
Mrs Baillie's Sunflower and Honey
    Squares 148
Open Sesame Slice 158
Orange Honey Creams 159
Pooh's Peanut Crisps 174

icing
Butter Icing 243
Chocolate Butter Icing 243

Chocolate Glacé Icing 241
Coffee Glacé Icing 241
Fruit Butter Icing 243
Fruit Glacé Icing 241
Glacé Icing 241
Vienna Icing 244

jam and marmalade
Apricot Almond Slice 17
Apricot Meringue Slice 25
Blackberry Lattice Fingers 33
Chocolate Jam Slice 61
Cinnamon Orange Squares 71
Fresh Berry Slice 85
Jam Bars 121
Jam Fancies 122
Maria's Easy-peasy Biscuits 139
Old English Matrimonials 155
Raspberry Drops 179
Sara's Apricot Slice 187

lemon
Apricot, Ginger and Lemon Slice 20
Auntie Ruth's Lemon Slice 28
Glazed Lemon Jumbles 102
Lebkuchen 129
Lemon Fluff Slice 130
Lemon Jelly Layer Squares 132
Lemon Rice Biscuits 65
Lemon Sponge Biscuits 134
Swiss Lemon Slice 216
Yoghurt Bars 236

marshmallow
Lemon Fluff Slice 130
Maraschino Marshmallow Slice 138
Marshmallow Fingers 140
Rocky Road 184
Rose Royal Slice 185
meringue
Apricot Meringue Slice 25
Macadamia Meringue Squares 137
Meringues 143

nuts
American Tollhouse Cookies 11
Apricot Hazelnut Crunch 22
Banana Nut Biscuits 30
Chocolate Nut Florentines 64
Currant Granola Squares 81
Florentine Bars 84
Fruity Cereal Bars 88
Georgian Baklava 90
Hazelnut Crescents 108
Macadamia Meringue Squares 137
Mum's Chocolate Walnut Slice 150
Nut Drops 227
One-pot Brownies 156
Orange Thins 161
Peanut Crunch Biscuits 170
Peanut Slice 171
Pooh's Peanut Crisps 174
Rocky Road 184
Scrummy Six-layer Slice 192
Spicy Slice 207
Sugared Brazil Bars 210
Treacle Flapjacks 223
Walnut Whiteys 228
see also almonds

oats
Anzac Biscuits 13
Anzac Slice 14
Jennifer's Flapjacks 123
Oatcake Crackers 154
Old English Matrimonials 155
Open Sesame Slice 158
Parkin 162
Scottish Oatcakes 191
Shona's Midnight Munchies 197
Sydney Specials 217
orange
Anzac Slice 14
Cinnamon Orange Squares 71
Orange Drops 227
Orange Honey Creams 159
Orange Rice Biscuits 65

Orange Thins 161

passionfruit
Passionfruit Biscuits 164
Passionfruit Cream-cheese Slice 166
Passionfruit Fingers 169

sesame seeds
Apricot and Sesame Slice 19
Open Sesame Slice 158
Sesame Potato Biscuits 194
Sesame Snack Bars 195
Sweet Sesame Biscuits 215
shortbread
Almond Shortbread 8
Billionaire Shortbread Bars 32
Cinnamon Ginger Shortbread 198
Ginger Shortbread 198
Korzhiki (Russian Shortbread) 127
Posh Choc-shortbread Squares 176
Rich Chocolate Shortbread Crescents 182
Shortbread 198
spice
Abernethy Biscuits 1
Animal Biscuits 12
Anise Biscotti 4
Brandy Snaps 36
Caraway Crisps 44
Cinnamon Ginger Shortbread 198
Cinnamon Macaroons 68
Cinnamon Mince Slice 70
Cinnamon Orange Squares 71
Cinnamon Sugar Bars 72
Hodge Podge 113
Lebkuchen 129
Nutmeg Cannonballs 153
Orange Thins 161
Sesame Snack Bars 195
Spiced Jumbles 205
Spicy Apple Slice 206
Spicy Slice 207
Treacle Snaps 225
see also ginger

PENGUIN BOOKS

Published by the Penguin Group
Penguin Group (Australia)
250 Camberwell Road, Camberwell, Victoria 3124, Australia
(a division of Pearson Australia Group Pty Ltd)

New York Toronto London Dublin New Delhi Aukland Johannesburg

Penguin Books Ltd, Registered Offices: 80 Strand, London, WC2R 0RL, England

First published by Penguin Group (Australia), 2007

10 9 8 7

Many thanks go to Freedom Furniture in South Yarra, Matchbox in Armadale,
and Roost in Armadale, who provided a selection of the beautiful props.

Design by Claire Tice © Penguin Group (Australia)
Photographs by Julie Renouf, assisted by Renee Shepherd
Written by Victoria Heywood
Food styling by Julie Lanham and Linda Brushfield
Typeset by Post Pre-Press, Brisbane, Queensland
Scanning and separations by Splitting Image P/L, Clayton, Victoria
Printed in China by Everbest Printing Co. Ltd

National Library of Australia
Cataloguing-in-Publication data:

 Biscuit & slice bible.
 Includes index.
 ISBN 978 0 14 300585 8 (pbk.).
 1. Biscuits.

 641.815

penguin.com.au